KNITTI

The author, Winifred Butler, first learnt to knit when she was seven years old, and is now well-known and respected as a knitting expert. She was knitting editor of *Woman* for over twenty-four years and has also written many books including *Start to Knit* and *Start to Crochet* and *Better Knitting* for schools.

Winifred Butler has made frequent radio broadcasts and appeared on television, passing on the learning of a lifetime to beginners and teachers alike.

TEACH YOURSELF BOOKS

KNITTING

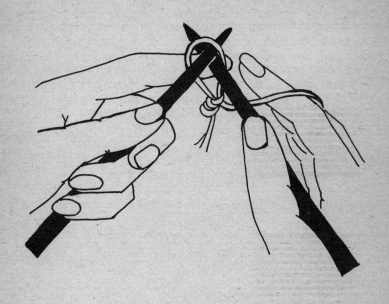

Winifred Butler

TEACH YOURSELF BOOKS
Hodder and Stoughton

First printed 1979
Copyright © 1979
Winifred Butler

British Library Cataloguing in Publication Data

Munro, Winifred
    Teach yourself knitting.
    1. Knitting
    I. Title
    746.4'32   TT820

ISBN 0–340–24661–8

Printed and bound in Great Britain for Hodder and
Stoughton Paperbacks, a division of Hodder and
Stoughton Limited, Mill Road, Dunton Green,
Sevenoaks, Kent, (Editorial Office; 47 Bedford
Square, London WC1 3 DP), by Richard Clay
(The Chaucer Press) Ltd, Bungay, Suffolk

Contents

Preface

This is a comprehensive guide to knitting. Starting with the basics which the absolute beginner needs, it goes on to cover all those points on techniques and care of materials and renovations which the experienced knitter needs to achieve the professional standard that is all-important.

The fundamentals of knitting are in fact very simple – all patterns, however complicated, have been built up from two basic stitches, knit and purl. It is the way these stitches are used and combined which gives the patterns and variety of modern knitwear.

Today, hand-knitting is high fashion all round the world. Here you will find the patterns for classic jumpers and cardigans for all the family which do not date, but once you have had some practice, you should be able to adapt these classics to incorporate modern details. A classic baby outfit and patterns for home furnishing are also included.

All patterns have been given in a full range of sizes and a table of international measurements, weights and yarn equivalents has been included for those who do not live in the UK.

1 Equipment

Only a few basic essentials are required for knitting, but these must be of the right kind to give the best results. In particular it is important to know the qualities of the different types of yarn and to know what knitting needles are available.

Yarns

The yarn is basic to your knitting and needs to be chosen with care. The main choice is between wool, cotton and man-made fibres, all of which come in different thicknesses, textures and mixtures. The ply means the number of strands that have been twisted together, and does not determine the thickness of the basic yarn. Always buy branded yarn – it is false economy to use inferior qualities. Good quality yarns last longer and are more satisfactory all round.

With such a variety of different yarns there is a danger of choosing the wrong type of yarn for a particular need. Double knitting thickness is the most used and consequently the most readily available in a wide range of colours. It is quick to knit and can be used for any type of garment, big or small. Creped yarn has a crisp texture and its high twist makes it hardwearing for a suit or a dress. Nubbly yarns are popular because they produce a textured fabric without the effort of working a fancy stitch. Finer yarns such as 2 and 3 ply for gossamer knitting and 4 ply for twin-sets etc. are available in a more restricted colour range. All these thicknesses come in pure wool and mixtures which are explained here.

Wool – Natural fibre which is warm and comfortable to wear. Wool has a springy texture which guarantees a good retention of shape. Some wool is treated with silicone to make it machine-washable, and this also reduces the 'pilling' (the small lumps which occur on the surface of the knitting with wear, due to the softness of pure wool). Wool comes in bright or muted colours, but it is not always fast to bright sun, and fading can occur.

Man made fibres – The three main fibres are nylon, acrylic and triacetate.

Nylon – Being a white fibre, nylon can be dyed radiant colours. It dries quickly because the moisture content is low. It can be very warm to wear being non-porous and is preferable when blended with wool or acrylic.

Acrylic – This fibre produces Courtelle, Orlon and Acrilan. These are high bulk yarns, but lightweight, so they give more yardage per ball. Colours are fast to light and they are easy to wash and dry – suitable for baby knitting.

Triacetate – Blends of tricel and nylon make the yarn silky in appearance. It is machine-washable and crease resistant.

Angora – A soft fluffy yarn from the Angora rabbit. It stretches easily and also tends to shed, so care should be exercised in selecting the right design. Pale Angora cannot be worn over black clothes. As Angora is expensive it is sometimes used only to accent knitting, such as for edgings or a collar, or for tiny party boleros.

Mohair – A luxurious yarn from the Angora goat. It is best knitted on large needles to show the furriness to advantage. Because of this, it tends to stretch and care must be taken in washing. It is extremely warm and suitable for outdoor wear.

See page 108 for equivalent yarns in America, Australia and South Africa. Also a conversion guide for quantities.

Pure new wool

Figure 1

This symbol is used internationally to mark pure new wool. Otherwise the yarn constituents are specified on the ball band and the label carries special symbols for ironing, cleaning, etc. It is important to read the symbols correctly at the making-up stage as these have been incorporated after careful research by the manufacturers to give the best results.

Dye lots – Be sure to check these are the same on all the ball bands. Shades vary from one dye to another, and even though they may not be noticeable in the ball they will show up distinctly in the knitted fabric.

Knitting needles

These must be undamaged, with good points, to produce perfect work. They are made in three lengths, 25 cm (10 in), 30 cm (12 in) and 35 cm (14 in), and are sold in pairs with knobs on the end to hold the stitches in place. Use the length that suits you best – some people prefer the shortest needles, even if it means bunching up large numbers of stitches, whilst others prefer the longest needles, which are tucked under the arm. Double-pointed needles are sold in the same lengths in sets of four. The shorter ones are used for seamless knitting, such as socks and gloves, and for any narrow bands.

Circular needles, for knitting seamless 'tubes', can also be used for flat pieces of knitting, turning at the end of each row, and knitting backwards and forwards instead of in a circle. They are available in several lengths from 40 cm (16 in) to 100 cm (42 in) lengths. It is essential to use the right length, and it must not be longer than the circular measurement being knitted, as the stitches have to stretch from point to point. Circular needles are often used when more stitches than can be accommodated on straight needles are involved.

Cable needles are very short, and double-pointed, used for holding a few stitches at a time in the process of moving these to left or right for the cable pattern twist. It is preferable to use a smaller-size needle than the knitting needle being used for the same piece of work – if the stitches are stretched on to needles which are too large they are likely to be distorted.

Needle gauge – This is a gauge which measures needle sizes and is essential for checking needle sizes when the numerals are illegible or missing. The needles must fit the numbered hole or notch exactly. See page 107 for international equivalents.

Tape measure – This is most useful if it has centimetres and inches given parallel on each side so that comparison is quick and easy. Buy a firm, good quality tape measure which will not stretch and become inaccurate.

Ruler – This is ideal for measuring short distances on the straight.

Wool needle – This is used for making up. It has a large eye for threading yarns and a blunt point that will not split the knitted fabric.

Pins – Use long steel ones for blocking, i.e. pinning the knitted sections out to their measurements before pressing – they will not leave rust marks on the dampened fabric.

Buttons – Choose these according to the weight of the yarn used. They should not be heavier than the knitted fabric, or they will stretch it out of shape. Buttons should be slightly larger than the buttonhole to hold fastened. Buttons with shanks allow for the buttoned-on layer, but alternatively 'stems' of yarn can be made (see page 16).

Zip fasteners come in many lengths and weights. Match these as near as possible to the yarn, and if the exact colour is unobtainable choose a darker shade to blend. The pattern will specify the length and type of zip needed. Closed-end zips rise by 2·5 cm (1 in) in the 10 to 25·5 cm (4 to 10 in) lengths, then by 5 cm (2 in) for the 25·5 cm to 66 cm (10 to 26 in) lengths; open-end zips (for jackets) rise by 5 cm (2 in) from 25·5 cm to 66 cm (10 to 26 in) lengths.

Workbag – It is very helpful to have a roomy one to keep everything together – yarn, needles, tape measure, pattern and any buttons bought for the garment. This will save a lot of frustration.

2   How to read a pattern

Always read all the instructions given before the cast-on stage. Vital information can easily be missed if introductory details are ignored.

Materials

Under this heading is listed the yarn for the garment and the needles with which it is to be knitted. Also any trimmings needed. Always use the yarn recommended, because this is what will produce the right effect – do not be tempted to use apparently interchangeable qualities as these vary in thickness and length from one spinner to another.

Measurements

An extra allowance is made on actual body measurement – this is for movement, and varies from 2·5 cm (1 in) on fine baby clothes to 15 cm (6 in) on bulky garments. For instance the 86 cm (34 in) instructions work out to actual measurement of 91·5 cm (36 in). Half this garment will measure 46 cm (18 in). The length given is up to the beginning of the shoulder shaping. The sleeve is always the underarm measurement.

Tension

This is the key to all knitting being the right shape and size, and a guarantee that everything knitted will be completely satisfactory. No two people knit the same way, and it is essential to get the prescribed tension exactly right before starting on the pattern.

Work a sample with the recommended yarn and needles, big enough to measure the tension in the centre, so that the edge stitches do not have to be included (these tend to distort and give inaccurate measurements). Remove needle or cast off, and place the sample on a flat surface.

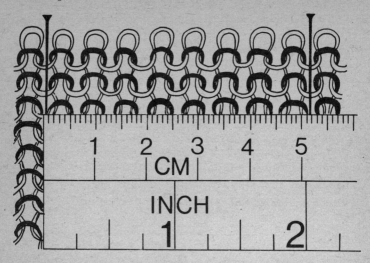

Figure 2

Mark the stitches with pins, as shown in Figure 2, and measure carefully.

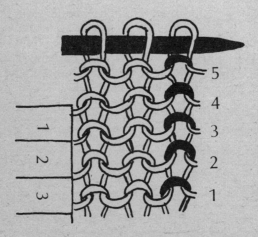

Figure 3

Most pieces of knitting have two obvious sides – when counting rows, count these on the ridged side. One ridge is one row. For gather stitch, which is the same on both sides, each ridge counts as two rows (Figure 3).

If your sample does not measure up to the given tension, change needle sizes and start again. If there are too few stitches the knitting is too loose so change to a smaller size needle. If too many stitches it is too tight, so change to a larger size needle. Keep on changing needle sizes until the tension is exactly right – this will make sure you do not have to undo your knitting and re-knit at a later stage. It is no good thinking that a difference of half a stitch or one stitch won't matter, because these stitches add up to a considerable number over the entire garment. For example:

> Take 222 stitches as sufficient for a size 86 cm (34 in) garment.
> Tension of 12 stitches to 5 cm (2 in) will work out to 90·05 cm (36 in).
> Tension of 13 stitches to 5 cm (2 in) will work out too small at 85 cm (33½ in).
> Tension of 11 stitches to 5 cm (2 in) will work out too large at 100 cm (40 in).

The same happens with rows:

> 224 rows at 16 rows to 5 cm (2 in) will give a length of 70 cm (28 in).
> 224 rows at 17 rows to 5 cm (2 in) will only measure 66 cm (26 in).

Getting the right number of stitches to the cm is more important than keeping to the recommended size of needles, so do not start the pattern until the tension is right.

When measuring work in progress place the tape in a straight line, ignoring shapings. It is helpful to mark the first row of armhole shaping so that the later measurements can easily be made from this line. (Figure 4).

Abbreviations

It is necessary to use abbreviations to save repetition, and most terms are easily recognisable. A list of abbreviations most commonly used is given below. Some patterns have special abbreviations for cabling and twisting and these are always fully explained within the pattern. *It is important to read any abbreviations before starting to knit from instructions.*

K. – knit; p. – purl; st(s). – stitch(es); beg. – beginning; inc. – increase: by working into front and back of next stitch; dec. – decrease: by

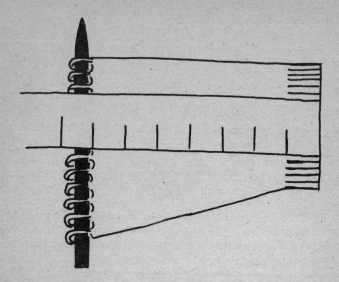

Figure 4

working 2 stitches together; rep. – repeat; tog. – together; sl. – slip; y.r.n. – yarn round needle: used to make a stitch between a knit stitch and a purl stitch, or between two purl stitches, taking yarn from the front of the work; y.fd. – yarn forward: used to make a stitch between two knit stitches, bringing yarn under the needle to the front of work and taking it over the needle to the back of work to knit next stitch; y.o.n. – yarn over needle: used to make a stitch between a purl and a knit stitch, taking yarn over the needle from front to back of work; p.s.s.o. – pass slip stitch over; g.st. – garter stitch; st.st. – stocking stitch; m.st. – moss stitch; M.C. – main colour; C. – contrast; cm(s) – centimetre(s); in(s) – inch(es); t.b.l. – through back loop; k.1.b. – knit 1 below (see page 57); t.2.1. – twist 2 left; t.2.r. – twist 2 right; m.1. – make 1; c.r. – cable right; c.l. – cable left; y.b. – yarn back.

Other abbreviations for individual patterns, such as C. for cable, are explained in the relevant instructions.

Comparative terms

England	America
England	*America*
Cast off	Bind off
alternate rows	every other row
tension	gauge
slip	skip
work straight	work even
stocking stitch	stockinette stitch
shape 'top'	shape 'cap'

Sizing

Instructions are given for the smallest size, with larger sizes in brackets. This means that the stitches to be worked are given in size order – the smallest size first, and remaining sizes in ascending order within brackets. If the pattern says k.8 (10:12) sts., this is 8 for the smallest size, 10 for the second size and 12 for the third size. Where only one figure is given it applies to all sizes.

Brackets

The instructions inside brackets must be worked the number of times stated immediately after the brackets, or until the given number of stitches remain on the left-hand needle.

A pattern repeat of four stitches over fourteen stitches could be given as '(k.2, p.2) 3 times, k.2' **or** '(k.2, p.2) to last 2 sts., k.2'.

Asterisks

Take care to repeat from the * to the semi-colon the number of times stated – if the pattern says 'repeat from * 6 times', the instructions from * to semi-colon must be worked 7 times in all.

Sometimes a combination of brackets and asterisks are used – necessary when bracketed instructions do not apply to all of the pattern repeat. To take fourteen stitches again, a pattern could be given as '*K.2, (k.1, p.1.) twice; repeat from * once, k.2'. **or** *K.2, (k.1, p.1.) twice; rep. from * to last 2 sts., k.2'.

Making up

It is essential to take time and trouble doing this properly. It will make all the difference to the look of the finished garment. Very often beautifully knitted garments are ruined by hurried making up. This must be done step-by-step for it to be satisfactory.

Check the details on the yarn ball-band as some mixtures must not be ironed.

Blocking   (pinning the knitted sections out before pressing)

Do this on an even-padded surface, right side down, with steel pins.

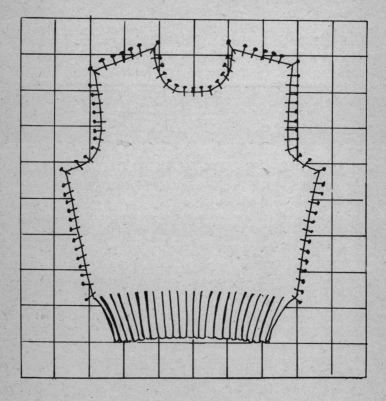

Figure 5

If possible use a checked cloth and this will make it easier to pin the sections out straight. Pin work every 2·5 cm (1 in). Do not pin ribbed sections. Check measurements with a tape measure at this stage. Use a warm iron over a damp cloth to press the work, omitting ribbed sections. Leave the knitting pinned until all the steam has evaporated. Block each section in this way (Figure 5).

Picking up stitches

This can make or mar a garment and unsightly holes must be avoided.

When picking up stitches around the neck or armhole shaping to knit collars or armbands, insert needle one stitch in from the very edge, avoiding distorted stitches (Figure 6).

Figure 6

Assembly

Use a wool needle, making seams on the wrong side. Be sure to match patterns or stripes throughout.

Use hairpins to hold edges together for sewing. These will not dislodge like pins (Figure 7).

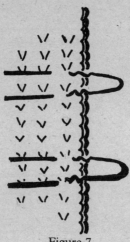

Figure 7

Joining seams

Back stitch
This is the strongest method of joining seams. Work from right to left and sew through the same line of knitting as far as possible (Figure 8).

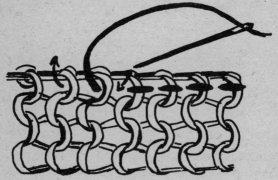

Figure 8

Join shoulder seams first, then set in sleeves (Figure 9).

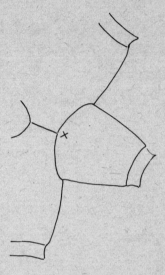

Figure 9

Match centre of sleeve top to shoulder seam and ease the sleeve top into the armhole. Assembly in this way allows for pressing the set-in sleeve seam on the flat. Join side and sleeve seams, oversewing ribbed sections.

Bulky yarns
Figure 10 shows oversewing through the knobs ('pips') formed at the edge of the knitted fabric. This is more suitable than back stitch for joining pieces together when bulky yarns are involved.

Darn all joining ends into seams for about 2·5 cm (1 in) then cut off excess. Press all seams on the wrong side.

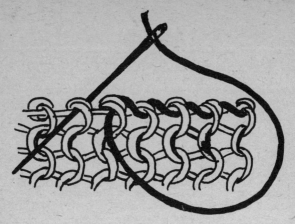

Figure 10

Woven seams

Figure 11 shows how to make an invisible seam. Weave from the right side,

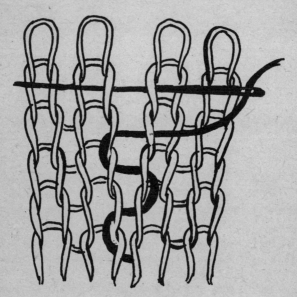

Figure 11

alternating from side to side for every stitch and drawing the thread up loosely.

Pocket linings

Pocket linings or patch pockets must be slip stitched lightly, matching stitch for stitch in a straight line – it is all too easy to slant stitches sideways and spoil the final appearance of the garment. To slip stitch, insert wool needle through a knitted loop on the main section then through a loop at the edge of the lining and draw thread up loosely.

Front bands

These should be slightly stretched when being pinned into position for sewing. Slip stitch loosely to avoid a puckered seam.

Herringbone casing

This holds elastic firmly in place for waist bands of skirts or dresses. The elastic should be 2·5 cm to 4 cm (1 to 1½ in) wide. Cut elastic to fit waist and join into a circle. With matching yarn work herringbone stitch from left to right around the inside of the garment, stitching above and below the elastic alternately to encase it (Figure 12).

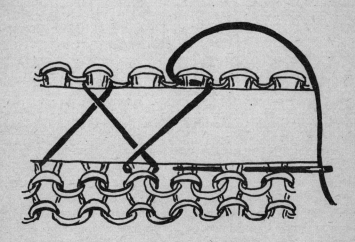

Figure 12

Fastenings

Zip fasteners

Before putting in the zip oversew the opening edges of the knitting together with contrast yarn. This will avoid stretched and uneven edges. Place the well stretched closed zip behind the oversewing and tack it into position, folding in the ends of the zip tape. Back stitch each side of the zip neatly, then remove tacking and oversewing (Figure 13).

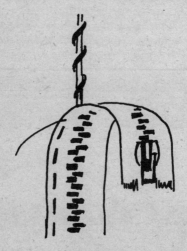

Figure 13

Buttons

There must be sufficient room underneath the button to allow for the thickness of the buttoned-on layer. If shank buttons are unavailable, make a stem as you sew the button on – stitch over a pencil or a knitting needle (Figure 14), then remove it and wind the yarn around the loose strands to form the stem.

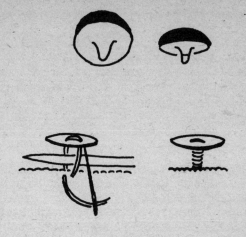

Figure 14

Preventing stretching

Taping seams

This will prevent stretching of seams in heavyweight garments. Fold straight binding over seams and slip stitch each side or back stitch through the binding as well when sewing seams.

3 How to knit

This chapter explains the complete process of knitting in detail, from casting on at the beginning to casting off at the end. It covers how to knit and purl, and different ways of increasing and decreasing. Use the basic patterns given in this chapter to practise and perfect the two basic stitches until you can achieve the knitted-by-an-expert look.

Use a thick yarn and large knitting needle to learn and compare what is being worked with the step-by-step diagrams. Also, limit the number of stitches as shown so that these can be counted frequently – it is very easy to make an extra stitch, or lose one, when learning to knit.

Note for left-handed workers

To follow the instructions, read left for right and right for left. Work each row from left to right.

To follow the diagrams, place a mirror to the right of the diagram, at right angles, and the illustrations will be reflected to the correct position for working left-handed. Reverse the procedure for decreases, k.2 tog.t.b.l. instead of k.2 tog. and vice versa. (See abbreviations page 8.)

To begin

Hold the yarn in the left hand and the needle in the right hand. Take the needle over and under the yarn to form a loop over the needle (Figure 15). Wind the continuous yarn around the point of the needle (Figure 16).

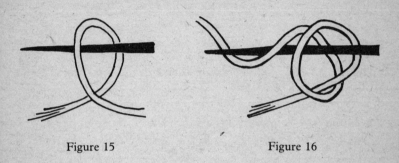

Figure 15   Figure 16

Draw the wound yarn through the original loop (Figure 17).

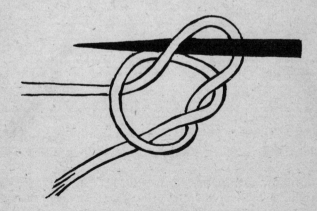

Figure 17

Figure 18

Pull the end of the yarn up to form a slip knot below the first stitch on the needle (Figure 18).

To cast on

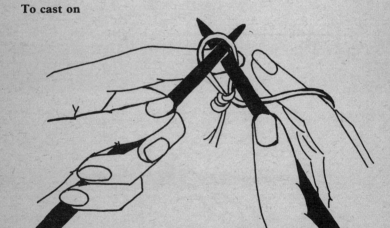

Figure 19

Hold the needle with the first stitch in the left hand. Take the second needle in the right hand. Insert the point of the right needle through the first stitch, underneath the left needle and to the left of the strand on the right of the needle (Figure 19).

Figure 20

Push the right-hand needle through to the back of the work. Wind the continuous yarn under and over the right-hand needle (Figure 20).

Figure 21

Draw the wound yarn through the first stitch with the point of the right-hand needle, forming a loop stitch on the needle (Figure 21).

Figure 22

Insert the point of the left-hand needle through the second stitch (Figure 22).

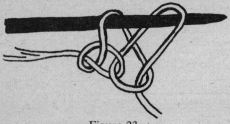

Figure 23

Slip the second stitch on to the left-hand needle, making two stitches (Figure 23).

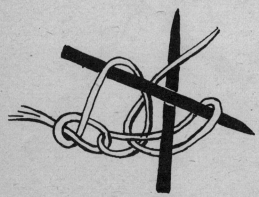

Figure 24

Insert right-hand needle between the two stitches on the left-hand needle. Wind yarn around needle and draw loop through the space for

each new stitch required. Make all the stitches evenly because a neat edge
is very important (Figure 24).

This method of casting on has been chosen because it gives a firm edge,
and there's no need for the tedious follow-up of working through the back
loops of stitches.

To knit

Hold the needle with the cast on stitches in the left hand. Keep the yarn
at the back of the work. Insert the right-hand needle through the first
stitch and pass yarn under and over the point of the needle (Figure 25).

Draw the wound yarn through the stitch, making a loop on the right-
hand needle. Drop the stitch off the left-hand needle. This completes one
knitted stitch (Figure 26).

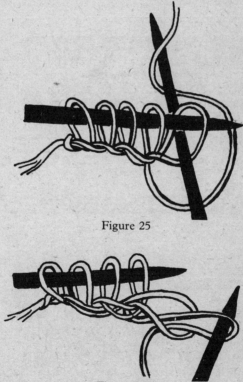

Figure 25

Figure 26

Knit each stitch in this way to the end of the row (Figure 27).

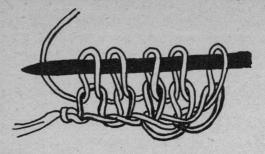

Figure 27

The other side of the knitted row forms a ridge – shown dark in Figure 28.

Figure 28

Knit all the rows in the same way as the first row, taking the stitches off the left-hand needle on to the right-hand needle, for each row (Figure 29).

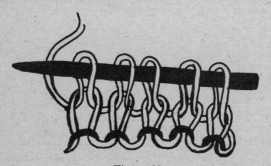

Figure 29

This is called *garter stitch* (or 'plain' knitting). It is the very first stitch learnt in knitting, and consists solely of the basic 'knit 1' that occurs throughout all knitting patterns. There is no right or wrong side, so it is ideal for reversible things. It has a springy texture so must be patted into shape before being measured. When counting garter stitch rows remember that each 'ridge' marks two rows (Figure 30).

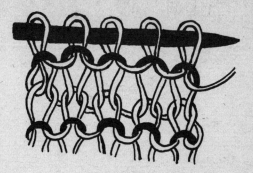

Figure 30

Casting off

As well as being used to finish off work, casting off is used to decrease several stitches at a time for armhole and neck shapings, and buttonholes.

Keep the cast off stitches as loose as the knitted fabric. If there's a tendency to tighten up in casting off, use a larger needle for this.

Casting off knitwise

Knit 2 stitches, with point of the left-hand needle lift the first knitted stitch over the second and off the needle (Figure 31).

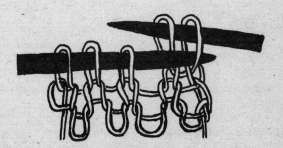

Figure 31

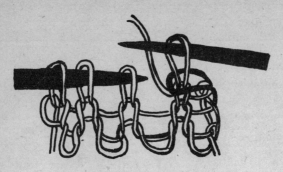

Figure 32

One stitch remains on the right-hand needle after casting off. This stitch must be counted in with the stitches on the left-hand needle for continuation of pattern (Figure 32).

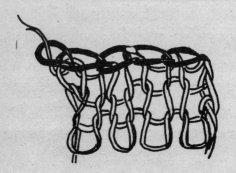

Figure 33

Continue casting off in this way (knitting 1 more stitch each time) until 1 stitch remains on the right-hand needle. Draw yarn through this stitch to fasten off (Figure 33).

Now that the basic principle of knitting is understood, it should be possible to make a whole garment. The very first thing that is successfully knitted and completed is the most exciting project and it is also the best ever encouragement to continue the good work.

Striped sweater (Figure 34)

This pattern is especially for beginners and a most comfortable sweater to wear. It is all one piece of plain (garter stitch) knitting, with no shaping or fancy stitches – only a neck opening as shown in the diagram. Instructions are given for four colours to make it more interesting to knit, but it can be made all in one colour if preferred, or in any available oddments of double knitting.

Figure 34

The pattern

Materials   Lister/Lee Target Superwash Double Knitting – 7 (25 g)
balls in each of four colours: two 4½ mm (No. 7) knitting needles.
Measurements   To fit 81 cm (32 in) bust; length, 66 cm (26 in); cuffed
sleeve, 38 cm (15 in).
Tension   10 stitches and 19 rows to 5 cm (2 in).

Front   Cast on 90 stitches. Using all four colours in turn knit 17-row
stripes until 10 stripes have been worked. Cast on for the sleeves but
continue to change colour every 17 rows.
Sleeves   Cast on 90 stitches at beginning of next 2 rows. Continue until
16th row of 5th sleeve stripe has been worked on these 270 stitches.
Neck opening   Knit 112, cast off 46 stitches, knit to end. *Next row*   Knit
112, cast on 46 stitches, knit to end. Complete 5 more stripes on these
stitches. Cast off 90 stitches at beginning of next 2 rows.
Back   Work 10 stripes. Cast off.

Making up

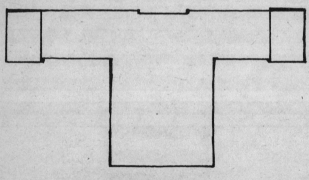

Figure 35

Fold garment in half and join side and sleeve seams (see page 13) then
turn back sleeves to form cuffs (Figure 35).

To purl

Keep the yarn at the front of the work.

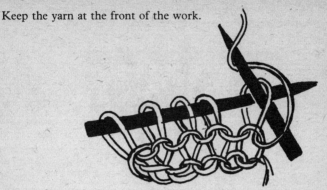

Figure 36

Insert right-hand needle through stitch from right to left and wind yarn around point of needle (Figure 36).

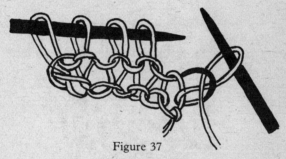

Figure 37

Draw wound yarn backwards through the stitch, making a loop on right-hand needle. Drop the stitch off left-hand needle (Figure 37).

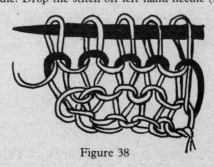

Figure 38

Purl each stitch in this way to the end of the row (Figure 38).

Alternate rows of knit and purl make stocking stitch – the most widely used stitch. All the classics on page 68 are mainly in stocking stitch.

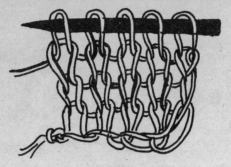

Figure 39

On one side the surface is flat, showing rows of linked loops (Figure 39).

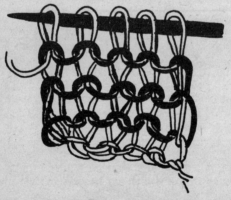

Figure 40

On the other side the surface is ridged, shown by the darkened loops (Figure 40).

Casting off purlwise

Purl 2 stitches, then take yarn to back of work before lifting first stitch over second. Continue in this way for the number of stitches to be cast off.

Both knit and purl cast off is used when casting off in rib (k.1, p.1 etc.), or in pattern (comprised of both k. and p. in varying numbers), working stitches as they fall, either knit or purl, and moving the yarn to the back of work before casting off the purled stitches.

Decreasing

There is more than one way of reducing the number of stitches, and it is essential to work the correct method for the right effect, especially in lacy patterns.

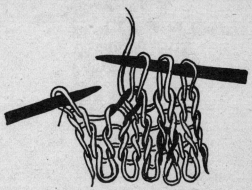

Figure 41

Knit 2 stitches together (k.2 tog.)   Insert needle through next 2 stitches, from left to right, and draw the yarn through both stitches at the same time. Drop both stitches off left-hand needle, leaving one stitch on right-hand needle. The decreased stitch will slant to the right.

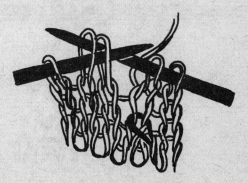

Figure 42

Knit 2 stitches together through back loop (k.2 tog.t.b.l.)   Insert needle through next 2 stitches, from right to left, and draw yarn through both stitches at the same time. Drop both stitches off the left-hand needle, leaving one stitch on right-hand needle. The decreased stitch will slant to the left.

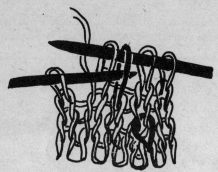

Figure 43

Slip 1, knit 1, pass slipped stitch over (sl.1, k.1, p.s.s.o.)   To slip a stitch, pass it from one needle to the other without knitting it – insert right-hand needle through next stitch from right to left (purlwise) and pass it on to right-hand needle without working into it, k.1, then lift the slipped stitch over the knitted stitch with the point of the left-hand needle. The decreased stitch will slant to the left.

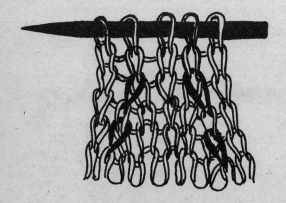

Figure 44

Fully Fashioning The decreased stitches must fall in opposite directions (Figure 44) and the methods are explained in Figures 41, 42 and 43.

Purl 2 stitches together (p.2 tog.) Insert needle from right to left through the next 2 stitches and draw the yarn (as for purl) back through both stitches at the same time.

Purl 2 stitches together through back loops (p.2 tog.t.b.l.) Loosen next 2 stitches with the point of the right-hand needle first. Insert needle from left to right, from back of work, through next 2 stitches and draw the yarn (as for purl) back through both stitches at the same time.

Increasing

There are different ways of increasing the number of stitches, and it is essential to work the correct method – as specified in the particular pattern being worked.

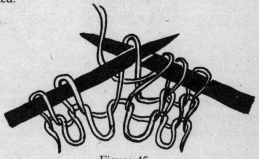

Figure 45

Increase 1 stitch (inc. 1 st.) *in knit stitch* Work twice into the same stitch. First knit into the front of the stitch in the usual way but do not drop stitch off left-hand needle, knit into back of the same stitch (Figure 45).

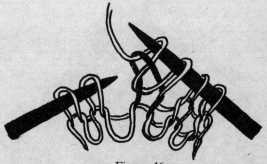

Figure 46

Drop the stitch off the left-hand needle, leaving the increased stitch on the right-hand needle (Figure 46).

To increase in a purl stitch, work into the front of the stitch purlwise, then loosen the same stitch on the left-hand needle by drawing it back with the point of the right-hand needle, before purling into back loop (Figure 47).

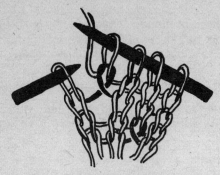

Figure 47

Make 1 (m.1)   This is made between stitches. Insert right-hand needle under the horizontal strand preceding the next stitch and lift it up on to the left-hand needle. Knit or purl into the back of this looped yarn to increase one stitch (Figure 48).

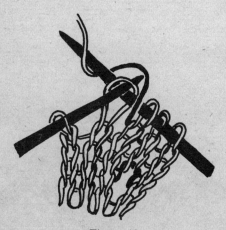

Figure 48

Yarn forward (y.fd.)   This method is used to form a hole between stitches. To increase in this way between knit stitches, bring yarn forward between needles and take it back over the right-hand needle before knitting the next stitch (Figure 49).

Figure 49

Yarn over needle (y.o.n.)   This refers to an increase between a purl and a knit stitch. After purling a stitch, take the yarn over the right-hand needle before knitting the next stitch.

Yarn round needle (y.r.n.)   To increase between 2 purl stitches – after purling a stitch, take the yarn over and under the right-hand needle back to the front of the work in place to purl the next stitch.

Moss stitch

This is a combination of knit and purl stitches to form a reversible knitted fabric (Figure 50).

Figure 50

The pattern

The pattern must be worked over an uneven number of stitches. Knit 1, *bring yarn forward between needles, purl 1, take yarn back between needles and knit 1; repeat from * to end of row (Figure 51).

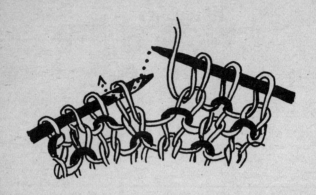

Figure 51

In moss stitch the knit and purl stitches must be alternated in every row. A wrongly worked stitch will disrupt the entire row and it is as well to check from time to time that the pattern is working out correctly.

Practise moss stitch until it is absolutely even and make the practice pieces into something useful afterwards. Work in strips, or squares, and use small scraps to stripe these to add interest. Remember to join new yarn at the beginning of rows – knot ends and darn these into the seams afterwards.

Strips

Use double knitting yarn and two 3¾ mm (No. 9) knitting needles. Cast on 7 stitches for a 2·5 cm (1 in) width, 13 stitches for a 5 cm (2 in) width, 19 stitches for 7·5 cm (3 in) or 37 stitches for a 15 cm (6 in) width. Work in moss stitch for the length required then cast off.

Squares

Cast on as for strips but fold knitting diagonally (whilst it is still on the needle) and when the side edge is the same as the lower (cast on) edge, cast off in pattern.

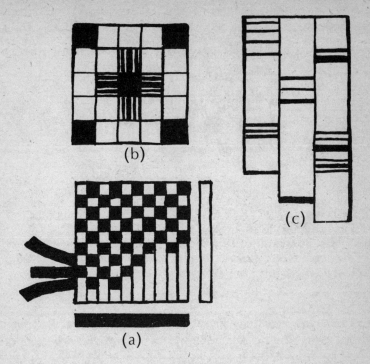

(b)

(c)

(a)

Figure 52

(a) Figure 52 shows 2·5 cm (1 in) wide strips in contrasting colours interwoven to make a firm fabric for a cot or pram cover.

(b) 5 cm (2 in) plain and striped squares arranged to form a patterned cushion cover.

(c) 7·5 cm (3 in) strips made from oddments, being joined to make a cover for a doll's pram, or a double bed, depending on how much practice is needed to make the knitting perfect.

Ribbing

This is used to give the necessary elasticity to welts (waist bands), cuffs and collars. It consists of vertical columns of knit and purl stitches, which can be varied in width by the number of stitches alternated (Figure 53).

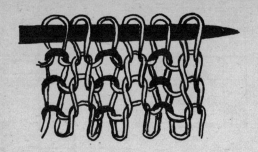

Figure 53

Single rib (k.1, p.1)   Knit 1, purl 1 alternately to the end of the row. In successive rows be sure to knit the previously purled stitch, and purl the previously knitted stitch, to keep the stitches in ribs of knit and purl.

Now practise rib by knitting a small scarf – it will use about 3 (25 g) balls of double knitting and 4 mm (No. 8) knitting needles.

Child's scarf pattern
Cast on 40 stitches and work in knit 1, purl 1 rib until the scarf measures about 80 cm (31½ ins). Cast off ribwise (knitting and purling alternately).

Adult's scarf pattern
5 (25 g) balls double knitting. Cast on 54 stitches and work in knit 1, purl 1 rib until the scarf measures 114 cm (45 in). Cast off ribwise.

Double rib (k.2, p.2)   Work knit 2, purl 2 to the end of the row. In successive rows be sure to knit the 2 stitches previously purled and purl the 2 stitches previously knitted, to keep the double ribs in line. As long as this principle is adhered to, any number of stitches divisible by 2 can be worked (Figure 54).

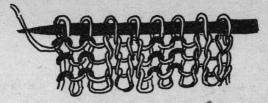

Figure 54

Wide rib

Any width of rib can be worked, varying from even numbers of knit and purl stitches to odd numbers such as k.1, p.2, forming a narrow knit rib and a wider purl rib. Alternatively this type of rib can also be used on the k.2, p.1 side where there will be a wide knit rib and a narrow purl rib (Figure 55).

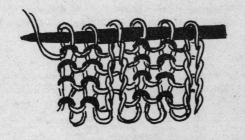

Figure 55

Useful hints

Tough thread

When there is no give whatsoever in the yarn being used, and stitches have to be worked together, loosen these first by levering them forward for knitting (back for purling) with the other needle.

Turning rows

Sometimes, when shaping, certain numbers of stitches are left unworked at the end of the row – unless the pattern states otherwise, slip the first stitch on each return row to make a neater turn.

Joining yarn

Never knot yarns in the middle of a row, as this would spoil the look of the work and weaken the knitted fabric. Always join at the side, and darn in ends afterwards.

Winding yarn

This must be done very loosely. Avoid all pressure or stretching as this would destroy the elasticity in the yarn. Wind yarn over fingers and release the loops alternately.

Circular knitting

Be especially careful when knitting the very first round after casting on and make sure the cast on stitches have not twisted around the needle. If you do not notice a twist you will have to pull the knitting right back to the beginning.

Contrast edgings

Use the main colour to pick up the stitches then change to the contrast – this will avoid a jagged line, especially around shaped edges.

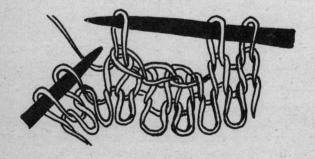

Figure 56

Buttonholes (Figure 56)

The stitch remaining on the right-hand needle after casting off the required number of stitches must be counted in for continuity of the pattern.

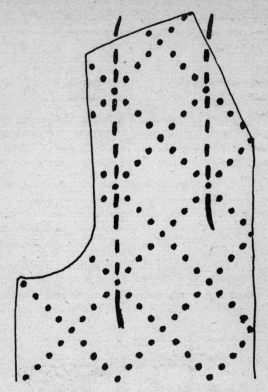

Figure 57

Pattern markers (Figure 57)

Shaping in lace patterns can be very difficult. Mark the beginning and end of complete pattern repeats with contrast yarn when any shaping is in progress – this will ensure alignment in continuity of the pattern. Carry the contrast thread in and out of rows to separate the odd stitches involved.

Edges

Sewing up is made easier if the first stitch is slipped and the last stitch knitted on every row – this forms 'pips' that can be matched when seaming.

Cable knitting

Use a contrast thread (or safety pin) to mark the ridge on the wrong side of the cable row – this will make it easy to count the number of rows to the next cable.

Yarn shortage

If in doubt regarding the amount of yarn available to complete a garment, work both sleeves together and the yarn limitation will decide to what length the sleeves can be made.

Casting on

For heavy-duty garments use yarn double to give extra strength. For yarns with no give, such as cotton and nylon, use a larger size needle to lend elasticity.

Striped knitting

If the stripes are not too wide, carry the yarn not being used loosely up the side of the work and this will save darning in ends afterwards.

Dropped stitches

When this happens it is usually possible to pick the dropped stitch up row-by-row, using a crochet hook. This saves unravelling the work. Choose a smaller size crochet hook than the knitting needle being used – this will prevent the fabric being stretched, and make it easier for the loose strands to be drawn through the loops (Figures 58a and 58b).

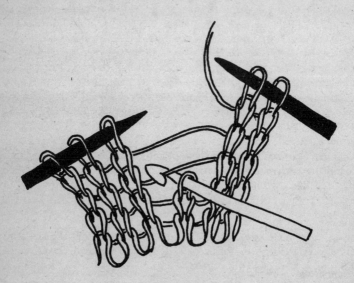

Figure 58a

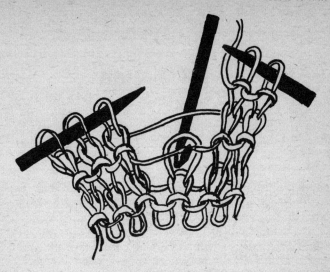

Figure 58b

(a) *Stocking stitch pattern* Insert the crochet hook through the dropped stitch loop from the front of the work and draw each strand (formed by the dropped stitch) through this loop in succession. Make sure that no strand is missed in the process. When all the stitches have been picked up in this way, transfer the final loop from the crochet hook on to the left-hand knitting needle.

(b) *Garter stitch pattern* Alternate from back to front of work. Insert the crochet hook from the back of the work, through the dropped stitch loop to draw the strands through purlwise, and from the front of the work to draw the strands through knitwise.

(c) *Lacy patterns* If a stitch is dropped it is best to catch the stitch with a safety pin (or contrast thread) then undo the knitting row by row, until the dropped stitch row is reached. In other words, it is easier to re-knit a lacy pattern than to put it right.

4 Additional techniques

Introducing different colours into your knitting gives great scope for patterning. This chapter shows you how to work stripes, both horizontal and vertical, and how to knit Fair Isle patterns. Another way to add colour is to embroider, or swiss darn, the knitted fabric, or to knit in beads or sequins. Interesting patterns can also be made in the knitting itself and cable twists, which are covered here, are a good example of this.

1 Striped knitting

Horizontal stripes

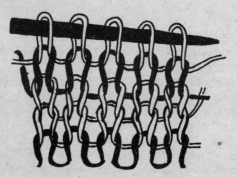

Figure 59 – Stocking stitch

Stocking stitch   The change to a contrast colour is done on a knit row to give an unbroken line on the right side of the work, but it can also be changed on the wrong side of the work if the first row with the new colour is purled. Stocking stitch is one row knit, one row purl (see page 30).

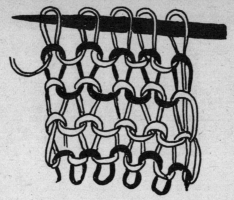

Figure 60

Reversed stocking stitch (the purl side of knit 1 row, purl 1 row)   This shows a broken line of overlapping main colour and contrast. This side of the work is used as the right side when a muted effect is preferred (Figure 60).

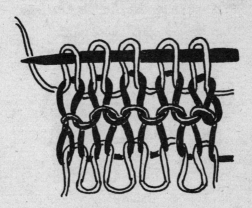

Figure 61 – Garter stitch

Garter stitch   Change to contrast colours from the same end of the work every time if a positive stripe is required. The other side of garter stitch stripes shows the broken line caused by the change of colour. Garter stitch is every row knit (see page 25).

Figure 62

This side of garter stitch is used as the right side when a muted effect is needed (Figure 62).

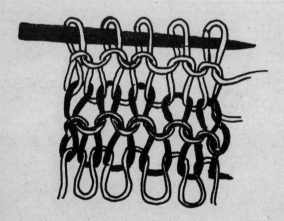

Figure 63

Two row stripes in garter stitch make one ridge in each colour (Figure 63).

Vertical stripes
To prevent holes when changing colours, interlock the yarns. Figures 64a and 64b are exaggerated so that the principle is clearly visible.

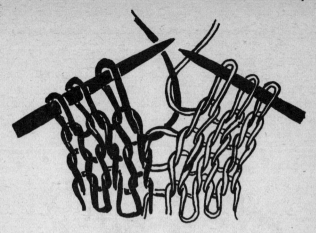

Figure 64a

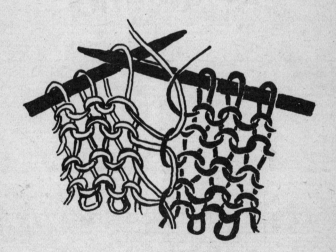

Figure 64b

(a) Shows the knit side row of vertical stripes

(b) Shows the purl side row of vertical stripes. The vertical stripes are knitted in stocking stitch.

2   Fair Isle

Fair Isle is knitting with two or more colours to form a design. There is always a tendency to work this too tightly, resulting in puckered knitting. Also, if the contrast yarn is woven in on the wrong side this tends to be unsightly on the right side – the colours do show through, however carefully this is done. The best method is to strand the yarns.

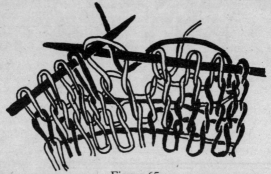

Figure 65

After working the required number of stitches in one colour, spread the worked stitches out on the right-hand needle and carry the next colour loosely behind these stitches before continuing the pattern – this will prevent puckering. For isolated motifs use separate balls of yarn for each colour (Figure 65).

Charts

These are easier to follow than row-by-row instructions in the pattern – it is also easier to check that the design being worked resembles that shown on the chart (Figure 66).

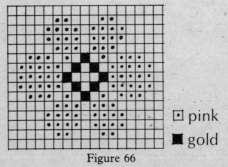

⊡ pink

■ gold

Figure 66

Each square in the chart represents one knitted stitch. Read knit rows from right to left and purl rows from left to right. Always work from the lowest line of the chart up to the top.

Sometimes a dotted line is used in charts when the motif is to be repeated, but this will be explained in the pattern – usually the dotted line separates the odd stitches to be worked at the end of the pattern repeat in the forward row, and at the beginning (before the repeats) of the return row.

Embroidery

It is possible to work the Fair Isle chart in cross stitch on the plain knitted fabric afterwards. Use the same thickness yarn for the embroidery so that it covers the knitted stitch adequately.

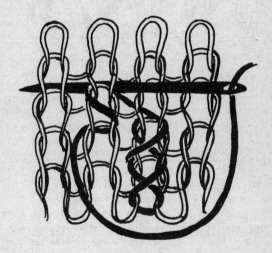

Figure 67

Following the Fair Isle chart, work one cross stitch over one knitted stitch (Figure 67).

3 Swiss darning

Another method of ornamenting plain stocking stitch. The alphabet chart on page 66 could be used in this way.

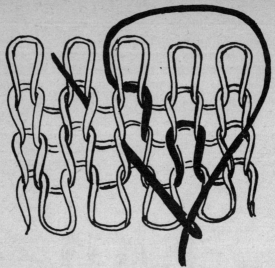

Figure 68

With contrast yarn in a wool needle, work directly over each knitted stitch, forming a second layer in the design (Figure 68).

4   Decorated knitting

Beaded knitting

Special beads, in different sizes, are available, with holes large enough to thread knitting yarn through. The beads are threaded on to the yarn before starting to knit, and the knitting pattern will give details of the bead size and the number of beads to be threaded on to each ball of yarn.

Figure 69a

(a) Spread the beads on a flat, non-shiny surface, pick up each bead in turn with the threaded sewing needle and slide the beads on to the knitting yarn (Figure 69a).

Figure 69b

(b) If the hole in the bead is too small to take the threaded sewing needle, fold a piece of fuse wire through the looped yarn and twist the wire to pass through the beads (Figure 69b).

Knitting with beads

Follow the pattern instructions for the placing of the beads. The beads are usually worked into alternate rows (Figure 70).

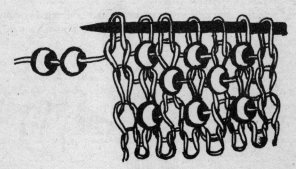

Figure 70

All-over pattern Cast on an uneven number of stitches. *1st row* *Knit 1, bring yarn forward and slip 1 stitch, move 1 bead up to the front of the slipped stitch, then take yarn to the back of the work; repeat from * to the last stitch, knit 1. *2nd row* Purl. *3rd row* Knit 1, repeat from * in 1st row to last 2 stitches, knit 2. *4th row* Purl. These 4 rows form the pattern and leave a bead-free stitch at each end of the knitting for the seam in making up.

Practice knitting with beads by making a small purse to sew on to a ready-made frame – a very rewarding exercise for one's own use, or to give as a gift. And it's fascinating to work too.

Sequin knitting

Sequins, like beads, vary in size. Be sure to obtain the size stated in the pattern.

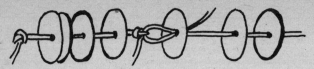

Figure 71a

(*a*) *Threading sequins* The type used for knitting are sold in strings of approximately 1000. These are transferred from the fine thread that holds them together on to the knitting yarn. The pattern will state how many strings are to be used per ball of yarn, and these are transferred by knotting the fine thread over the folded yarn and sliding the sequins on to the knitting yarn gently (so as not to break the thread and cause the sequins to scatter all over the place).

If a knot occurs in the knitting yarn, the already threaded sequins have to be re-transferred to new yarn beyond the knot. This means threading them back on to the fine yarn first (Figure 71a).

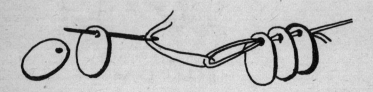

Figure 71b

(*b*) Large sequins, or paillettes as they are called, are only available separately, and the numbers specified in the pattern have to be threaded on to the knitting yarn individually. If the threaded knitting yarn is too thick to pass through the hole in the paillette, use a fine sewing needle and pass fine thread through the folded yarn before threading the double end through the eye of the needle (Figure 71b).

Knitting with sequins

The method for knitting small sequins is to pass one sequin at a time through the stitch as it is being worked. Move one threaded sequin up to the yarn that is being wound round the needle in the process of knitting the stitch, and push the sequin through the loop to the front of the work as the stitch is being completed (Figure 72).

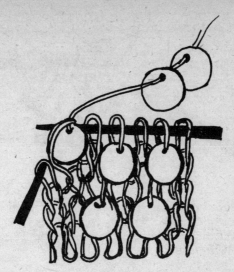

Figure 72

All over pattern with small sequins Cast on an uneven number of stitches. *1st row* Knit 1, *knit 1 sequin in next stitch, knit 1; repeat from * to end. *2nd row* Purl. *3rd row* Knit 2, *knit 1 sequin in next stitch, knit 1; repeat from * to last stitch, knit 1. These 4 rows form the pattern and leave a sequin-free stitch at each end of the knitting for the seam in making up.

Large sequins are attached to the work in different ways and these are explained in the pattern instructions. Generally they are moved up to the right side of the knitting when a wrong side row is being worked. They cannot be passed through the stitches as described for the small knitting sequins.

5 Cable knitting

This may look complicated, but is really not at all difficult. It consists of moving certain numbers of stitches over one another, to the left or right. A cable needle, which is quite short and pointed each end, is used for the cabling. Knitting patterns always give detailed instructions of the numbers of stitches to be used for the cable, which is usually done on the right side of the work, and the cabling is made more distinct by purling stitches each side of it.

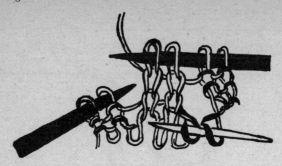

Figure 73a

(*a*) *Cable 4 left* Slip the next 2 stitches on to a cable needle and leave these at the front of the work. Work the next 2 stitches from the left-hand needle, then knit the 2 stitches from the cable needle. This completes the cable twist (Figure 73a).

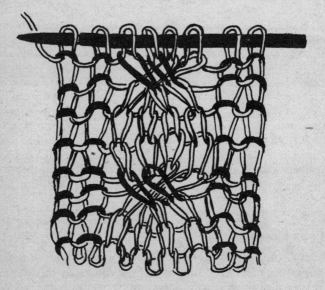

Figure 73b

(*b*) Two cables to the left have been completed, with 2 straight rows between (Figure 73b).

If cables are to be worked to the right, the stitches on the cable needle are held at the back of the work before knitting the next 2 stitches from the left-hand needle. Be sure to cable in the direction stated throughout the pattern. Otherwise beautifully knitted garments are often marred by irregular twists and wrong numbers of rows worked between the cabling.

On page 90 there is a bedspread made up of strips of cable patterns and it would make a good exercise for perfecting cabling in various directions.

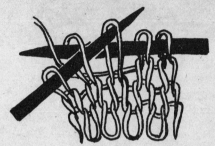

Figure 74a

(*a*) *Twist 2 left*   This can be done without the cable needle. Insert the needle through the back of the 2nd stitch on the left-hand needle, but do not slip the stitch off the needle (Figure 74a).

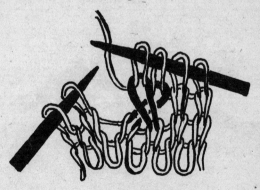

Figure 74b

(*b*)   Knit the first stitch from the front in the normal way, then slip both stitches off the left-hand needle together. This method twists 2 stitches to the left (Figure 74b).

If 2 stitches are to be twisted to the right, knit into the front of the 2nd stitch on the left-hand needle, but do not slip the stitch off, then knit into the first stitch and slip both stitches off the left-hand needle together.

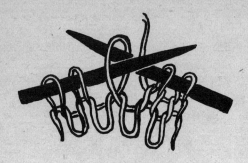

Figure 75a

(*a*) *Knit 1 through back loop* (k.1 t.b.l.)   Insert needle through loop of next stitch from behind left-hand needle (Figure 75a).

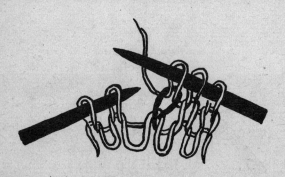

Figure 75b

(*b*)   When a stitch is knitted in this way it forms a twisted loop distinct from the normally knitted stitch. This technique is used to give a raised effect in patterns (Figure 75b).

Classic patterns for all the family.

Girl's fluffy cape.

Baby's angel top and shawl and knitted teddy bear.

Schoolgirl's waistcoat and cardigan.

Lacy sweater.

Sampler jumper.

Jacket.

Aran bedspread with cushions.

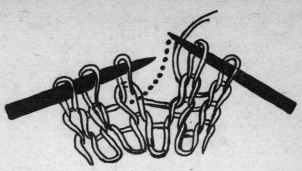

Figure 76a

(a) *Knit 1 below* (k.1.b.)   Used in Fisherman's rib and embossed honey-comb patterns, but illustrated here in stocking stitch for clarity. Insert needle through the loop below the next stitch on the left-hand needle, dropping the stitch above off the left-hand needle. Knitting one stitch into two rows at once lifts this stitch into relief (Figure 76a).

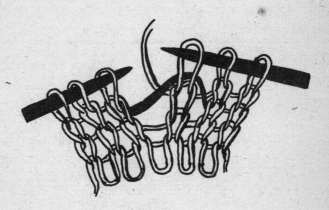

Figure 76b

(b)   When the stitch is knitted in this way a double-stranded stitch results (Figure 76b).

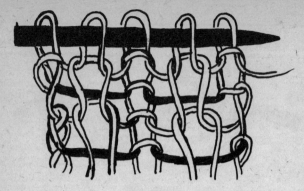

Figure 77

Slipped stitch rib   This entails slipping knit stitches on the right side rows and carrying the yarn behind the slipped stitches as shown (Figure 77).

5 Trimmings

A little trimming makes a lot of difference to the finish of a knitted fabric, whether a simple cord tie, a threaded ribbon, or a picot hem. Smocking on knitting is also effective or you can add initials or names to personalise knitting.

Cords

Use these to thread through welts that have stretched – to be drawn up and tied as required.

Cut strands three times the final length of cord. Tie one end firmly to a fixture and the other end to a pencil. Keep the yarn taut and hold the pencil vertically. Twist the pencil clockwise until the twists begin to knarl. Fold in the centre and allow the cord to twist round itself bit by bit. Knot ends. Make sure that cords are made thick enough – when they are too thin they tend to knot.

Knitted loop fringe

For abbreviations see page 8. Cast on 6 stitches. *Pattern row* (K.l, y.r.n., k.2 tog.) to end. Work the length required. *Next row* Cast off 3 stitches, fasten off. Drop the remaining stitches and unravel the knitting back to the beginning, forming a looped fringe.

Pompon

Cut two circles of required size and remove a third of the diameter from the centre (Figure 78).

Wind yarn around both cards until the centre hole is filled. Cut the outside edge, tie round the centre, between the cards, then remove the cards.

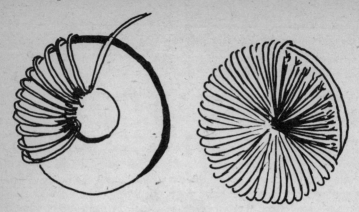

Figure 78

For a thinner pompon it is quicker to wind through the aperture on a half circle. Leave small extensions to hold the wound yarn in place. Lay a strand of yarn along the inside edge first, then wind over this until the inner half circle is filled. Cut along the outer edge and tie inside loops securely with the laid yarn (Figure 79).

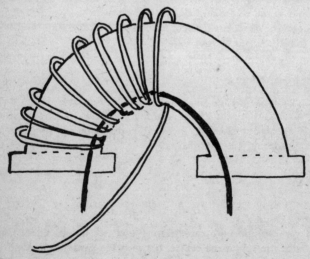

Figure 79

Tassel

(*a*)   Add several of these to trim scarves or cushions. Cut card to depth required. Lay yarn for tying along one edge. Wind yarn over card for thickness required (Figure 80a).

(*b*)   Tie top edge and cut lower edge. Bind around head of tassel to secure the loops. Always trim the ends (Figure 80b).

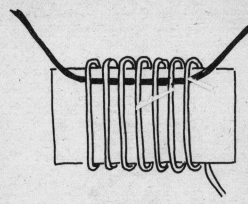

Figure 80a

Figure 80b

Fringing

Use a crochet hook and cut yarn (Figure 81).

(*a*) Fold yarn in half. Insert crochet hook through knitted fabric and draw folded end through.

(*b*) Keeping loop on stem of crochet hook, move hook up to wind cut ends around hook.

(*c*) Draw ends through loop already on hook.

(*d*) Pull ends to tighten loop to hold fringed ends.

Figure 81a

Figure 81b

Figure 81c

Figure 81d

Knotting

Take half the fringed strands from adjacent groups and knot them together. The illustration shows two rows of knots in the process (Figure 82).

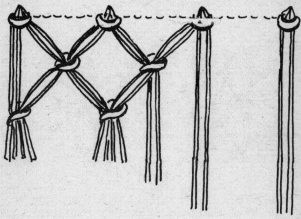

Figure 82

Ribbon slots

For each hole bring yarn forward and over needle (to make a stitch); then knit 2 together. Make an even number of holes for the ribbon to thread evenly to tie.

Picot hems

A row of holes (yarn forward, knit 2 together) on the fold-line of a stocking stitch hem forms the serrated edge that gives the effect of a picot edge.

Flower embroidery

Lazy daisy loop stitch petals, with french knot centres. Easy to work in plain yarn or mohair for a textured look (Figure 83).

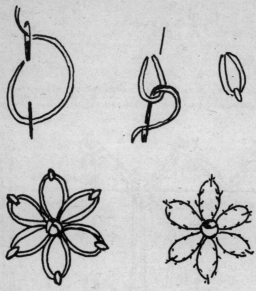

Figure 83

French knots   Wind needle around yarn and return needle where the thread was brought out (Figure 84).

Figure 84

Figure 85

Back stitch   This forms a continuous line on the surface and overlapped stitches underneath (Figure 85).

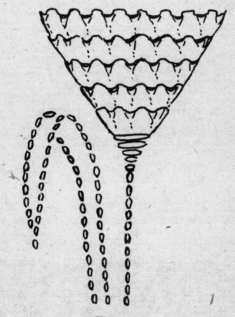

Figure 86

Carnation motif   This is quick and easy to apply to knitted fabric. Mark a triangle and gather narrow lace to fit this in layers. Add a calyx in straight stitch and work the stem and the leaf in back stitch (Figure 86).

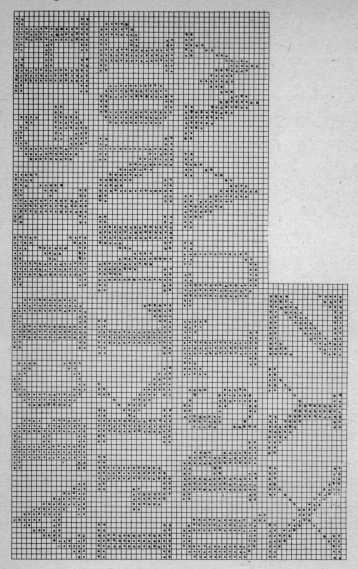

Figure 87

Alphabet   Each square on the chart represents one knitted stitch.

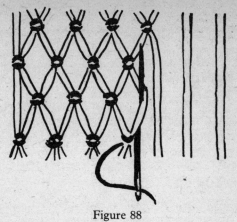

Figure 88

Honeycomb smocking

Work this over knitted rib in the same way as smocking is worked over pleated fabric. Take needle up and down alternately when sewing over two ribs – this will ensure that the elasticity is preserved (Figure 88).

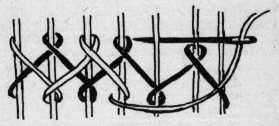

Figure 89

Herringbone smocking

Work two layers of herringbone stitch in contrasting colours over knitted rib. Follow the rows to keep the sewing in straight lines (Figure 89).

6 Patterns

(1) Classics

As the photograph on plate 1 shows, these classics cover a variety of styles giving you a wide choice. The jumpers can be made with a round or 'v' neck, or a polo collar, with or without sleeves. The cardigan is raglan sleeved, in high or low-button style. All these garments are given in basic stocking stitch and rib, but fancy stitches can easily be substituted for the stocking stitch, and patterns are included for basket, honeycomb, fisherman's rib, diagonal ridge, eyelet, trellis and rice stitch. All these stitches work to the tension prescribed for the classics, and the pattern repeats divide into the number of stitches required.

As double knitting yarn is available in lots of colours, two versions of the classics can be given a very different look – for instance, aubergine instead of pale blue, a mustard instead of a natural shade. Also, oddments of yarn could be used for striped versions.

In addition, the alphabet on page 66 can be used for initials or names to be knitted in or embroidered on afterwards.

Note: When several sizes are given in the one pattern (as for the classics) it can be exasperating to locate the number required at every stage. Before starting to knit underline all the numbers relating to the size required throughout the pattern – this will save time and obviate possible errors.

Knitted classics

Table of measurements and materials

Chest or Bust Sizes															
Cm	51	56	61	66	71	76	81	86	91	97	102	107	112	117
In	20	22	24	26	28	30	32	34	36	38	40	42	44	46
Garment Length Cm	27	30·5	35·5	40·5	46	51	56	58·5	61	63·5	66	68·5	71	73·5
In	10½	12	14	16	18	20	22	23	24	25	26	27	28	29
Sleeve Length Cm	19	23	28	33	38	39·5	40·5	42	43	44·5	46	47	48·5	49·5
In	7½	9	11	13	15	15½	16	16½	17	17½	18	18½	19	19½

Lister/Lee Target Double Knitting 25 g balls		7	9	11	13	15	16	17	18	19	20	21	22	23	24
Without Sleeves		5	6	8	10	12	12	13	13	14	14	15	16	17	18
Polo Collar	Add 1	1	1	1	1	1	1	2	2	2	2	2	2	2
Cardigan Buttons High	5	5	5	6	6	6	7	7	7	8	8	8	8	9
Low	3	3	3	4	4	4	5	5	5	6	6	6	6	7
Pockets	Add 1 ball to all quantities.														

(see plate 1)

Materials   Lister/Lee Target Double Knitting – see table above; two each 3¾ mm and 3¼ mm (Nos. 9 and 10) knitting needles.

Measurements   See table above.

Tension   12 sts. and 16 rows to 5 cm (2 in).

Abbreviations   See page 8.

Jumper

Back   With 3¼ mm (No. 10) needles cast on 66 (72:78:84:90:96:102: 108:114:120:126:132:138:144) sts. Work 2·5 (2·5:4:4:5:5:5:5:5:5:6:6:6:6) cm/1 (1:1½:1½:2:2:2:2:2:2:2½:2½:2½:2½) in k.2, p.2 rib. Change to 3¾ mm (No. 9) needles and continue in st.st. until work measures 15 (18:20:24: 28:32:36:37:38:39·5:40·5:42:43:44·5) cm/6 (7:8:9½:11:12½:14:14½:15:15½: 16:16½:17:17½) in, ending with a p. row.

Armhole shaping   Cast off 3 (3:3:3:3:3:6:6:6:6:6:6:6:6) sts. at beg. of next 2 rows *.

Dec. 1 st. at beg. of every row until 48 (52:56:60:64:68:78:82:86:90:94: 98:102:106) sts. remain**. Continue straight until work measures 27 (30·5: 35·5:40·5:46:51:56:58·5:61:63·5:66:68·5:71:73·5) cm/10½ (12:14:16:18:20: 22:23:24:25:26:27:28:29) in.

Shoulder shaping   Cast off 7 (7:7:8:8:8:8:9:9:9:9:10:10:10) sts. at beg. of next 4 rows for first six sizes and at beg. of next 6 rows for larger sizes. Leave remaining 20 (24:28:28:32:36:30:28:32:36:40:38:42:46) sts. on a stitch holder.

Front   As Back to **.

Round neck jumper (Figure 90)

Figure 90

Continue straight until work measures 21·5 (25·5:29:33:38:43:48:51:53·5: 56:58·5:61:63·5:66) cm/8½ (10:11½:13:15:17:19:20:21:22:23:24:25:26) in, ending with a p. row.

Neck shaping   Next row   K.19 (19:19:21:21:21:34:37:37:37:37:40:40: 40) sts., turn. Leave remaining sts. on a stitch holder. Continue on these sts. only *** dec. 1 st. at neck edge of next 5 (5:5:5:5:5:10:10:10:10:10:10:10: 10:10) rows. Continue straight until work measures 27 (30·5:35·5:40·5:46: 51:56:58·5:61:63·5:66:68·5:71:73·5) cm/10½ (12:14:16:18:20:22:23:24:25: 26:27:28:29) in, ending at armhole edge.

Shoulder shaping   Cast off 7 (7:7:8:8:8:8:9:9:9:9:10:10:10) sts. at beg. of next and following alternate row for first six sizes and following 2 alternate rows for larger sizes. Place centre 10 (14:18:18:22:26:10:8:12:16:20:18:22: 26) sts. on a stitch holder. Join yarn to inner edge of remaining sts. and complete to match other side from ***.

Sleeves   With 3¼ mm (No. 10) needles cast on 30 (30:36:36:42:42:48:48: 48:54:54:54:60:60) sts. and work 4 (4:4:5:5:5:5:5:6:6:6:7·5:7·5:7·5) cm/1½ (1½:1½:2:2:2:2:2:2½:2½:2½:3:3:3) in k.2, p.2 rib. Change to 3¾ mm (No. 9) needles and continue in st.st., inc. 1 st. at each end of every 4th row for first six sizes, and every 5th row for larger sizes, until there are 44 (44:50:

56:62:68:78:78:84:84:90:90:96:102) sts. Continue straight until work measures 19 (23:28:33:38:39·5:40·5:42:43:44·5:46:47:48·5:49·5) cm/7½ (9: 11:13:15:15½:16:16½:17:17½:18:18½:19:19½) in. Shape top by casting off 3 sts. at beg. of next 2 rows for first six sizes and 6 sts. at beg. of next 2 rows for larger sizes. Dec. 1 st. each end of every row until 14 sts. remain for first six sizes and 18 sts. remain for larger sizes. Cast off.

Neckband   Join right shoulder seam. With 3¼ mm (No. 10) needles, and right side facing, pick up and k.23 (23:25:31:31:31:42:44:42:40:40:44:42: 40) sts. down left edge of front neck, k. sts. from stitch holder at centre front, pick up and k.23 (23:25:31:31:31:42:44:42:40:40:44:42:40) sts. up right edge of front neck, k. sts. from stitch holder at centre back. 76 (84: 96:108:116:124:124:124:128:132:140:144:148:152) sts. ******** Work 2·5 cm (1 in) k.2, p.2 rib. Cast off ribwise.

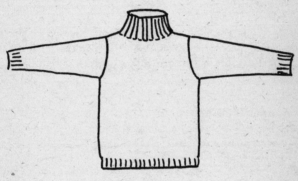

Figure 91

Polo collar (Figure 91)
As neckband to ******** Work 5 (5:6·5:6·5:7·5:7·5:7·5:10:10:10:12·5:12·5:12·5: 15:15) cm/2 (2:2½:2½:3:3:4:4:4:5:5:5:6:6) in k.2, p.2 rib. Cast off ribwise.

Sleeveless jumper (Figure 92)

Figure 92

Armbands   Join left shoulder seam. With 3¼ mm (No. 10) needles, and right side facing, pick up and k.60 (64:72:80:84:88:104:108:112:116:120: 124:132:136) sts. evenly around armhole edge. Work 2·5 cm (1 in) k.2, p.2 rib. Cast off ribwise.

V-neck jumper (Figure 93)

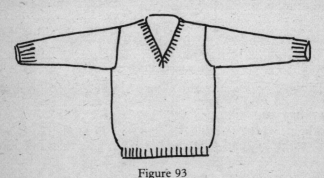

Figure 93

Work back, sleeves or armbands as for round neck jumper.

Front   As back of round neck jumper to * in armhole shaping.

Neck shaping   Next row   K.2 tog., k.28 (31:34:37:40:43:43:46:49:52:55: 58:61:64) sts., turn. Leave remaining sts. on a stitch holder. Continue on these sts. only, * dec. 1 st. at beg. of next 5 (6:7:8:9:10:5:6:7:8:9:10:11:12) alternate rows, *at the same time* dec. 1 st. at neck edge on every 3rd row until 14 (14:14:16:16:16:24:27:27:27:27:30:30:30) sts. remain. Continue straight until work measures 27 (30·5:35·5:40·5:46:51:56:58·5:61:63·5:66: 68·5:71:73·5) cm/10½ (12:14:16:18:20:22:23:24:25:26:27:28:29) in, ending at armhole edge.

Shoulder shaping Cast off 7 (7:7:8:8:8:8:9:9:9:9:10:10:10) sts. at beg. of next and following alternate rows for first six sizes and following 2 alternate rows for larger sizes. Join yarn to inner edge of remaining sts. and k. to end. Dec. 1 st. at beg. of next row then complete from * as other side.

Neckband Join right shoulder seam. With 3¼ mm (No. 10) needles, and right side facing, pick up and k.48 (52:56:60:64:68:64:68:72:72:76:80:84: 84) sts. down left edge of front neck, k.1 from centre by picking up horizontal strand at centre and knitting into back of it. K.48 (52:56:60: 64:68:64:68:72:72:76:80:84:84) sts. up right edge of front neck and k. sts. from stitch holder at centre back neck. Work 2·5 cm (1 in) k.2, p.2 rib, dec. 1 st. each side of centre front st. on every row. Cast off ribwise.

Making up Press work. *Jumper with sleeves:* Join left shoulder and neckband or polo collar seam. Set in sleeves. Join side and sleeve seams. *Sleeveless jumper:* Join side and armband seams. Press seams.

Button-up cardigan with raglan sleeves (Figure 94)

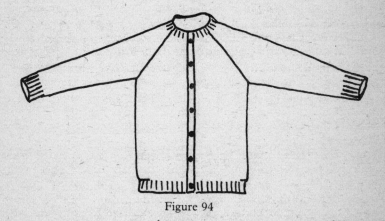

Figure 94

Back With 3¼ mm (No. 10) needles cast on 66 (72:78:84:90:96:102:108: 114:120:126:132:138:144) sts. Work 2·5 (2·5:4:4:5:5:5:5:5:5:6:6:6:6) cm/1 (1:1½:1½:2:2:2:2:2:2:2:2½:2½:2½:2½) in k.2, p.2 rib. Change to 3¾ mm (No. 9) needles and continue in st.st. until work measures 16·5 (19:23:26·5:30·5:

34:38:39·5:40·5:42:43:44·5:46:47) cm/$6\frac{1}{2}$ ($7\frac{1}{2}$:9:$10\frac{1}{2}$:12:$13\frac{1}{2}$:15:$15\frac{1}{2}$:16:$16\frac{1}{2}$: 17:$17\frac{1}{2}$:18:$18\frac{1}{2}$) in, ending with a p. row. *

Note Do not slip edge stitches for raglan shaping as this would make the seam too tight.

Raglan shaping Cast off 6 sts. at beg. of next 2 rows then dec. 1 st. at beg. of every row until 20 (22:24:26:28:30:30:32:34:36:38:40:42:44) sts. remain. Cast off.

Left front With $3\frac{1}{4}$ mm (No. 10) needles cast on 30 (36:36:42:42:48:48: 54:54:60:60:66:66:68) sts. Work as Back to *.

Raglan shaping Cast off 6 sts. at beg. of next row then dec. 1 st. at beg. of every alternate row until 12 (18:15:21:19:24:18:22:20:24:22:26:24: 26) sts. remain.

Neck shaping Cast off 1 (3:3:4:2:5:2:6:3:8:6:9:8:9) sts. at beg. of next row. First six sizes: dec. 1 st. at beg. of every row until 1 st. remains. Fasten off. For larger sizes dec. 1 st. at neck edge on next 8 (8:9:8:8:9:8:9) rows, *at the same time* continue raglan shaping as before until 1 st. remains. Fasten off.

Right front As left front, reversing shapings by ending with a k. row before *.

Sleeves With $3\frac{1}{4}$ mm (No. 10) needles cast on 30 (30:36:36:36:42:48:48: 48:54:54:54:60:64) sts. Work 4 (4:4:5:5:5:5:5:6:6:6:7·5:7·5:7·5) cm/$1\frac{1}{2}$ ($1\frac{1}{2}$: $1\frac{1}{2}$:2:2:2:2:2:$2\frac{1}{2}$:$2\frac{1}{2}$:$2\frac{1}{2}$:3:3:3) in k.2, p.2 rib. Change to $3\frac{3}{4}$ mm (No. 9) needles and continue in st.st., inc. 1 st. each end of every 4th row for first six sizes, and every 5th row for larger sizes, until there are 52 (56:60:64:68: 72:82:86:90:94:98:102:106:110) sts. Continue straight until work measures 19 (23:28:33:38:39·5:40·5:42:43:44·5:46:47:48·5:49·5) cm/$7\frac{1}{2}$ (9:11:13:15: $15\frac{1}{2}$:16:$16\frac{1}{2}$:17:$17\frac{1}{2}$:18:$18\frac{1}{2}$:19:$19\frac{1}{2}$) in. Shape raglan as Back until 6 sts. remain for first six sizes and until 10 sts. remain for larger sizes. Cast off.

Neckband Join raglan seams. With $3\frac{1}{4}$ mm (No. 10) needles, and right side facing, pick up and k.78 (82:86:90:94:98:102:106:110:114:118:122: 126:130) sts. evenly around neck. Work 2·5 cm (1 in) k.2, p.2 rib. Cast off ribwise.

Buttonhole band With $3\frac{1}{4}$ mm (No. 10) needles, cast on 10 sts. Work in k.2, p.2 rib. Work 1·5 (2:2:·5:2:1·5:2:2:·5:2:·5:2:·5:2) cm/$\frac{1}{2}$ ($\frac{3}{4}$:$\frac{3}{4}$:$\frac{1}{4}$:$\frac{3}{4}$:$\frac{1}{2}$:$\frac{3}{4}$: $\frac{3}{4}$:$\frac{1}{4}$:$\frac{3}{4}$:$\frac{1}{4}$:$\frac{3}{4}$:$\frac{1}{4}$:$\frac{3}{4}$) in. *Next row* (make buttonhole) Rib 4, cast off 2, rib 4. *Next row* Rib 4, cast on 2 sts., rib 4. Continue making 4 (4:4:5:5:5:6:6:6: 7:7:7:7:8) more buttonholes 5 (5·5:7:7·7·5:8:7·5:8:9:7·5:8:8:9:9) cm/2 ($2\frac{1}{4}$ $2\frac{3}{4}$:$2\frac{3}{4}$:3:$3\frac{1}{4}$:3:$3\frac{1}{4}$:$3\frac{1}{2}$:3:$3\frac{1}{4}$:$3\frac{1}{4}$:$3\frac{1}{2}$:$3\frac{1}{2}$) in apart, measured from base of previous buttonhole. Work 1·5 (2:2:·5:2:1·5:2:·5:·5:2:·5:1·5:·5:1·5) cm/$\frac{1}{2}$ ($\frac{3}{4}$:$\frac{3}{4}$:$\frac{1}{4}$:$\frac{3}{4}$:$\frac{1}{2}$: $\frac{3}{4}$:$\frac{1}{4}$:$\frac{1}{4}$:$\frac{3}{4}$:$\frac{1}{4}$:$\frac{1}{4}$:$\frac{1}{4}$:$\frac{1}{2}$) in. Cast off ribwise. Work other band to match, omitting buttonholes.

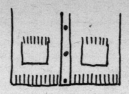

Figure 95

Pockets   With 3¾ mm (No. 9) needles cast on 18 (18:24:24:30:30:30:30:30: 30:36:36:36:36) sts. Work 5 (5:7·5:7·5:10:10:10:10:10:10:12·5:12·5:12·5: 12·5) cm/2 (2:3:3:4:4:4:4:4:4:5:5:5:5) in in st.st. Change to 3¼ mm (No. 10) needles and work 2·5 cm (1 in) k.2, p.2 rib. Cast off ribwise.

Low buttoning cardigan with raglan sleeves (Figure 96)

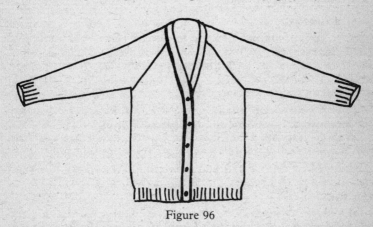

Figure 96

Back, sleeves and pockets   As button up cardigan.
Left front   As button up front to raglan shaping.
   Raglan and front shaping   Cast off 6 sts., k. to end. **First six sizes:** Dec. 1 st. at beg. of next and every 3rd row until 10 (6:11:7:12:8) sts. remain, *at the same time* dec. 1 st. at beg. of every alternate row (for raglan) until 1 st. remains. Fasten off. **Larger sizes:** Dec. 1 st. at beg. of next and every following 5th (4th:5th:4th:5th:4th:5th:5th) row until 6 (5: 5:5:4:5:3) sts. remain, *at the same time* dec. 1 st. at beg. of every alternate row (for raglan) until 1 st. remains. Fasten off.

Right front   As left front, reversing shapings by ending with a k. row before *.

Front band   Join raglan seams. With 3¼ mm (No. 10) needles, cast on 10 sts. Work in k.2, p.2 rib. Work 1·5 (1·5:2:2:·5:·5:1·5:·5:1·5:·5:1·5:2:·5: 1·5) cm/½ (½:¾:¾:¼:¼:½:¼:½:¼:½:¾:¼:½) in. *Next row* (make button hole)   Rib 4, cast off 2, rib 4. *Next row*   Rib 4, cast on 2, rib 4. Continue making 2 (2:2:3:3:3:4:4:4:5:5:5:5:6) more buttonholes 6·5 (7·5:9:7:9:10:8:9:9:7·5: 7·5:7·5:8:7) cm/2½ (3:3½:2¾:3½:4:3¼:3½:3½:3:3:3:3¼:2¾) in apart (measured from base of previous buttonhole). Continue in rib until band, when slightly stretched, will fit front edges and back neck. Cast off.

Making up   Press work. Join side and sleeve seams. Sew on front bands, placing buttonholes as required. Sew on pockets. Press seams. Sew on buttons to correspond with buttonholes.

Alternative stitch patterns

(1) **Basket stitch**   *1st row*   (K.3, p.3) to end. Rep. last row twice. *4th row*   (P.3, k.3) to end. Rep. last row twice. These 6 rows form patt.

(2) **Honeycomb stitch**   Use 4 mm (No. 8) needles because this stitch contracts. *1st row*   K.1, (k.1.b. [see page 57], k.1) to last st., k.1. *2nd row*   K. *3rd row*   K.2, (k.1.b., k.1) to end. *4th row*   K. These 4 rows form patt.

(3) **Fisherman's rib**   *1st row*   K. *2nd row*   K.1, (k.1.b. [see page 57], p.1) to last st., k.1. Rep. 2nd row throughout for patt.

(4) **Diagonal ridge**   *1st row*   (K.3, p.3) to end. *2nd row*   P.1, (k.3, p.3) to last 5 sts., k.3, p.2. *3rd row*   K.1, (p.3, k.3) to last 5 sts., p.3, k.2. *4th row*   (P.3, k.3) to end. *5th row*   P.2, (k.3, p.3) to last 4 sts., k.3, p.1. *6th row*   K.2, (p.3, k.3) to last 4 sts., p.3, k.1. These 6 rows form patt.

(5) **Eyelet**   *1st row*   P. *2nd row*   K.2, (y.fd., sl.1, k.2, p.s.s.o. last 2 sts.) to last st., k.1. *3rd row*   P. *4th row*   K. *5th row*   P. *6th row*   K.1, (sl.1, k.2, p.s.s.o. last 2 sts., y.fd.) to last 2 sts., k.2. *7th row*   P. *8th row*   K. These 8 rows form patt.

(6) **Trellis**   *1st row*   K.1, (y.fd., k.2 tog.) to last st., k.1. Rep. this row for patt.

(7) **Rice stitch**   *1st row*   (K.1, p.1) to end. *2nd row*   (K.1, p.1) to end. *3rd row*   (P.1, k.1) to end. *4th row*   (P.1, k.1) to end. These 4 rows form patt.

(2) Baby's angel top and shawl

An unusual lacy-peaked pattern is combined with plain knitting, to make a pretty pair (see plate 2b).

Angel top

Materials 7 (20 g) balls Lister Easy Wash Baby Double Knitting; two 3¼ mm (No. 10) knitting needles; 3 small buttons; 230 cm (90 in) narrow ribbon.

Measurements To fit 6 to 9 months; length, 27·5 cm (10¾ in); sleeve, 15 cm (6 in).

Tension 11 sts. to 5 cm (2 in) over g.st.

Abbreviations See page 8.

Main section ** Cast on 30 sts. K. 2 rows. *3rd row* (wrong side) K.6, (y.fd., k.2 tog.) 11 times, y.fd., k.2. *4th and every alternate row* K. *5th row* K.9, (y.fd., k.2 tog.) 10 times, y.fd., k.2. *7th row* K.12, (y.fd., k.2 tog.) 9 times, y.fd., k.2. *9th row* K.15, (y.fd., k.2 tog.) 8 times, y.fd., k.2. *11th row* K.18, (y.fd., k.2 tog.) 7 times, y.fd., k.2. *13th row* K.15, (y.fd., k.2 tog.) 9 times, y.fd., k.2. *15th row* K.12, (y.fd., k.2 tog.) 11 times, y.fd., k.2. *17th row* K.9, (y.fd., k.2 tog.) 13 times, y.fd., k.2. *19th row* K.6, (y.fd., k.2 tog.) 15 times, y.fd., k.2. (39 sts.) *21st row* K. *22nd row* Cast off 9 sts. loosely, k. to end. These 22 rows form patt. ** Rep. patt. twice then work 10 patt. rows.

Armhole shaping *11th row* Cast off 6, patt. to end. *12th row* K., cast on 6 sts. Continue in patt. until 10th row of 11th patt. has been worked. Rep. armhole shaping rows. Continue straight until 14 patts. have been completed. K.1 row. Cast off.

Sleeves Cast on 33 sts. K. 7 rows. P. 1 row (wrong side). *Eyelet row* K.1, (y.fd., k.2 tog.) to end. P.1 row. *Next row* K.1, (inc. in next st., k.1) to end. (49 sts.) Continue in g.st. until work measures 15 cm (6 in) from beg. To shape top cast off 3 sts. at beg. of next 2 alternate rows. Dec. 1 st. each end of next 2 rows. Leave 39 sts. on spare needle.

Yoke   With right side facing join yarn to centre back at straight edge of main section and pick up and k.45 sts. along edge to beg. of left armhole shaping, with right side facing k. sts. of one sleeve, pick up and k.84 sts. along front of main section, k. sts. of other sleeve, pick up and k.45 sts. along remaining top edge of main section (252 sts.) *Next row*   K.4, (p.2 tog.) 22 times, (p.2, p.2 tog.) 8 times, p.2, (p.2 tog.) 44 times, (p.2, p.2 tog.) 8 times, p.2, (p.2 tog.) 22 times, k.4. (148 sts.) *Eyelet row*   K.4, (y.fd., k.2 tog.) to last 4 sts., k.4. *Next row*   K.4, p. to last 4 sts., k.4. K. 2 rows. *Dec. row*   K.9, ★ (k.2 tog.) twice, k.10; rep. from ★ to last 13 sts., (k.2 tog.) twice, k.9. (128 sts.) ★★★ K. 1 row. *Next row* (make buttonhole) K.2, y.fd., k.2 tog., k. to end. K. 3 rows ★★★. *Dec. row*   K.8, ★ (k.2 tog.) twice, k.8; rep. from ★ to last 12 sts., (k.2 tog.) twice, k.8. K. 5 rows. *Dec. row*   K.7, ★ (k.2 tog.) twice, k.6; rep. from ★ to last 11 sts., (k.2 tog.) twice, k.7. rep. from ★★★ to ★★★. *Dec. row*   K.6, ★ (k.2 tog.) twice, k.4; rep. from ★ to last 10 sts., (k.2 tog.) twice, k.6. K. 5 rows. *Dec. row*   K.5, ★ (k.2 tog.) twice, k.2; rep. from ★ to last 9 sts., (k.2 tog.) twice, k.5. (48 sts.) Rep. from ★★★ to ★★★. Cast off.

Making up   Press lightly. Join sleeve seams. Join tiny underarm seams. Cut two 50-cm (19¾ in) lengths of ribbon. Thread them through eyelet rows of cuffs to tie at top. Cut remaining ribbon into two. Sew one end of each to end of eyelet row of yoke on wrong side, inside g.st. borders. Thread through eyelets to tie at centre front. Sew on buttons.

Baby's shawl

Materials   9 (20 g) balls Lister Easy Wash Baby 3 ply Knitting; two 3¼ mm (No. 10) knitting needles; 68·5 cm (27 in) narrow ribbon.

Measurements   91·5 cm (36 in) square.

Tension   12 sts. to 5 cm (2 in) over g.st.

Abbreviations   See page 8.

Centre   Cast on 1 st. Work in g.st., inc. 1 st. at beg. of every row until work measures 60 cm (23½ in) along side edge. Dec. 1 st. at beg. of every row until 1 st. remains. Fasten off.

Edging   Work as main section of Angel Top from ★★ to ★★ 60 times. Cast off.

Making up   Pin edging around centre, allowing 15 patts. to each side, pinning 11 patts. straight and gathering 4 to ease around corner. Oversew edging to centre and join ends neatly. Cut ribbon in two and sew bows to opposite corners of centre. Press lightly.

(3) Teddy in plain knitting

This is made from one piece of plain knitting (garter stitch). The pattern starts with the legs and continues with the body and arms in stripes, then the head (front and back which is folded in the centre when making-up the teddy), and finally the arms, body and legs again (Figure 97).

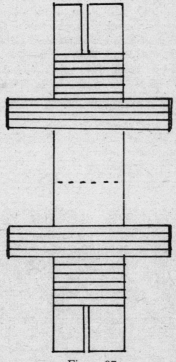

Figure 97

Materials   Double Knitting Wool – 1 ball (25 g) each gold, red and black; two 3¾ mm (No. 9) knitting needles; kapok for filling.

Measurement   32 cm (12½ in) tall.

Tension   11 sts. and 22 rows to 5 cm (2 in).

Abbreviations   See page 8.

Legs   ** With gold cast on 12 sts. K. 30 rows **. Leave these 12 sts. on safety pin. Rep. from ** to **. Break off gold. With red work across both sets of sts.

Body in stripes – * k. 4 rows red, 2 rows black. Rep. from * 4 times.

Arms   Continue in stripe patt. Cast on 12 sts. at beg. of next 2 rows. Work 18 rows on these sts. Cast off 12 sts. at beg. of next 2 rows. Break off red and black.

Head   With gold k. 60 rows. Break off gold.

Arms   With red, cast on 12 sts. at beg. of next 2 rows. K. 2 more rows. With black k. 2 rows. Work 14 rows stripe patt. Cast off 12 sts. at beg. of next 2 rows.

Body   Work 30 rows stripe patt. Break off black and red.

Legs   With gold, k. 12 sts., turn. Leave remaining sts. on a safety pin. K. 29 rows. Cast off. Rejoin yarn to remaining sts. K. 30 rows. Cast off.

Making up   Join top arm seams. With gold pick up and k.20 sts. along edge of arms. K. 3 rows. Cast off. Fold in half and join together inserting filling before closing seams. Sew across corners of head for 2·5 cm (1 in) for ears. Embroider mouth and eyes in black. Make a cord to thread around neck, and tie.

(4) Teddy in loop stitch

Knitted-in loops and soft mohair make this a very cuddly toy. The pieces are all knitted separately and joined together at the end.

Materials   6 (25 g) balls Mohair; two 3¾ mm (No. 9) knitting needles; scrap of black felt; two buttons with metal shanks for eyes; kapok for filling.

Measurement   38 cm (15 in) tall.

Tension   7 loop sts. to 5 cm (2 in)

Abbreviations   See page 8.

Body   Cast on 36 sts. K. 1 row. *1st patt. row*   (Insert needle into next st., wind yarn over needle then over index finger of left hand and round needle again, pull 2 loops through st., slip loop back on to left hand needle and k. them tog. with st. worked into through back of loop) to end. *2nd patt. row*   K., working double loops tog. Rep. last 2 rows 13 times. Cast off.

Legs (2)   Cast on 14 sts. ★ K. 1 row. Rep. 2 patt. rows 10 times. Cast off. ★

Arms (2)   Cast on 11 sts. K. 1 row. Rep. 2 patt. rows 8 times. Cast off.

Head   Cast on 32 sts. Rep. from ★ to ★ as legs.

Ears (2)   Use yarn double. Cast on 10 sts. K. 4 rows. K. 6 rows, dec. 1 st. at beg. of every row. Cast off remaining 4 sts.

Nose   Use yarn double. Cast on 27 sts. *1st and every alternate row*   K. *2nd row*   (K.3, k.3 tog., k.3) to end. *4th row*   (K.2 k.3 tog., k.2) to end. *6th row*   (K.1, k.3 tog., k.1) to end. *8th row*   (K.1, k.2 tog.) to end. K. 1 row. Cast off.

Making up   Join side and cast on seams of body. Fill. Join side and cast off seams of head. Fill and sew to body, gathering to form neck. From felt cut two 4 cm (1½-in) circles for paws and two 5 cm (2-in) circles for legs. Join side and cast off seams of legs and arms. Fill, then sew felt circles into openings. Sew legs and arms to body. Sew ears to head. Sew nose to head, filling firmly. Insert eyes through 2·5 cm (1-in) serrated felt circles (For infants, embroider eyes instead of using buttons). Sew to head. With black wool, embroider nose and mouth.

(5) Girl's cape

Made in soft, fluffy yarn this makes a perfect cover-up for a party dress. It is knitted all in one, mainly in reversed stocking stitch with garter stitch edgings and button fastening (see plate 2a).

Materials   8 (8:9) 25 g balls Lister's Tahiti Mohair; two each 3¼ and 4 mm (Nos. 10 and 8) knitting needles; 3 buttons.

Measurements   To fit 56 (61:66) cm/22 (24:26) in chest; length, 19 (23:26·5) cm/7½ (9:10½) in.

Tension   12 sts. and 15 rows to 5 cm (2 in).

Abbreviations   See page 8.

To make   With 3¼ mm (No. 10) needles cast on 262 (302:342) sts. Work 8 rows g.st. Change to 4 mm (No. 8) needles and work 6 rows st.st. *Next row*   *K.2, k.2 tog.t.b.l., k.20 (24:28), k.2 tog.; rep. from * 9 times, k.2. Work 5 rows st.st. *Next row*   *K.2, k.2 tog.t.b.l., k.18 (22:26), k.2 tog.; rep. from * 9 times, k.2. Continue in this way, working 2 sts. less between decs. on every 6th row until 142 (162:182) sts. remain, then dec. in the same way on every 4th row until 82 sts. remain. Work 3 rows. *Next row*   (K.2, k.2 tog.t.b.l., k.2, k.2 tog.) 10 times, k.2. Change to 3¼ mm (No. 10) needles and work 8 rows g.st. Cast off.

Front bands   With 3¼ mm (No. 10) needles cast on 5 sts. Work 42 (58:74) rows g.st. *Next row*   K.2, y.fd., k.2 tog., k.1. Work 2 more buttonholes 5 cm (2 in) apart. Work 4 rows g.st. Cast off. Make another band to match, omitting buttonholes.

Making up   Press lightly. Sew on front bands, making the reversed side of the stocking stitch on main part of the right side. Sew on buttons to correspond with buttonholes.

(6) Schoolgirl's waistcoat and cardigan

A snug-fitting, sleeveless, zipped waistcoat, with a casual long-line cardigan. Easy enough to be made by a schoolgirl, knitted mainly in stocking stitch and single rib (see plate 3a).

Materials Lister/Lee Target Motoravia 4 ply: Cardigan 16 (17:18) 25 g balls; Waistcoat 5 (6:7) 25 g balls; two each $3\frac{1}{4}$ mm and $2\frac{3}{4}$ mm (No. 10 and No. 12) knitting needles; 25·5 cm (10 in) open-end zip fastener.

Measurements To fit 76 (81:86) cm/30 (32:34) in bust; Cardigan-Length, 66 (68·5:71) cm/26 (27:28) in; sleeve, 42 (43:44·5) cm/$16\frac{1}{2}$ (17:$17\frac{1}{2}$) in; Waistcoat-Length, 42 (43:44·5) cm/$16\frac{1}{2}$(17:$17\frac{1}{2}$) in.

Tension 14 sts. and 18 rows to 5 cm (2 in).

Abbreviations See page 8.

Cardigan

Back With $2\frac{3}{4}$ mm (No. 12) needles cast on 116 (124:130) sts. Work 16 rows k.1 t.b.l., p.1 rib. Change to $3\frac{1}{4}$ mm (No. 10) needles and continue in st.st. until work measures 16·5 (18:19) cm/$6\frac{1}{2}$ (7:$7\frac{1}{2}$) in. Dec. 1 st. each end of next and every 12th row until 110 (118:124) sts. remain. Continue straight until work measures 47 (48:49) cm/$18\frac{1}{2}$ (19:$19\frac{1}{2}$) in.

Armhole shaping Cast off 9 sts. at beg. of next 2 rows, then dec. 1 st. at beg. of every row until 80 (86:90) sts. remain. Continue straight until work measures 66 (68·5:71) cm/26 (27:28) in.

Shoulder shaping Cast off 8 sts. at beg. of next 4 rows and 5 (7:8) sts. at beg. of next 2 rows. Cast off.

Left front With $2\frac{3}{4}$ mm (No. 12) needles cast on 64 (68:72) sts. Work 16 rows in k.1 t.b.l., p.1 rib. Change to $3\frac{1}{4}$ mm (No. 10) needles. *Next row* K. to last 16 sts., turn. Leave last 16 sts. on a safety pin. Continue in st.st., beg. with a p. row, until work measures 16·5 (18:19) cm/$6\frac{1}{2}$ (7:$7\frac{1}{2}$) in, ending with a p. row. Dec. 1 st. at beg. of next and every 12th row until 45 (49:53) sts. remain. Continue straight until work measures 43 cm (17 in), ending with a k. row.

Front shaping   Dec. 1 st. at beg. of next and every following 8th row until work measures 47 (48:49) cm/18½ (19:19½) in, ending p.

Armhole shaping   Still shaping front as set, cast off 9 sts. at beg. of next row, then dec. 1 st. at armhole edge on following 6 (7:8) alternate rows. Continue front shaping only until 21 (23:24) sts. remain. Continue straight until work measures 66 (68·5:71) cm/26 (27:28) in, ending p.

Shoulder shaping   Cast off 8 sts. at beg. of next and following alternate row. Work 1 row. Cast off.

Right front   As left, reversing front border sts. by leaving these on a safety pin at the beg. of row and working shapings at opposite ends to left front.

Pockets (2)   With 2¾ mm (No. 12) needles cast on 61 sts. Work 12·5 cm (5 in) in rib. *1st row*   K.1 t.b.l., (p.1, k.1 t.b.l.) to end. *2nd row*   P.1, (k.1 t.b.l., p.1) to end. Cast off ribwise.

Sleeves   With 2¾ mm (No. 12) needles cast on 54 (58:62) sts. Work 7 cm (2¾ in) in k.1 t.b.l., p.1 rib. Change to 3¼ mm (No. 10) needles and continue in st.st., inc. 1 st. each end of every 8th row until there are 72 (80:88) sts. Continue straight until work measures 42 (43:44·5) cm/16½ (17:17½) in. Shape top by casting off 9 sts. at beg. of next 2 rows, then dec. 1 st. at beg. of every row until 30 (34:38) sts. remain. Cast off 2 sts. at beg. of next 12 rows. Cast off.

Front borders   Join shoulder seams. Sl. 16 sts. on to 2¾ mm (No. 12) needles from safety pin and continue in rib as set until border fits front edge and across to centre back neck. Cast off.

Making up   Press work. Set in sleeves. Join side and sleeve seams. Sew on borders and join ends at centre back neck. Sew pockets to centre of each front 2·5 cm (1 in) above welt.

Waistcoat

Back   With 2¾ mm (No. 12) needles cast on 104 (112:118) sts. Work 10 cm (4 in) in k.1 t.b.l., p.1 rib. Change to 3¼ mm (No. 10) needles and continue in st.st. until work measures 25·5 cm (10 in).

Armhole shaping   Cast off 9 sts. at beg. of next 2 rows, then dec. 1 st. each end of next 4 (5:6) rows. Dec. 1 st. at beg. of every row until 68 (74:78) sts. remain. Continue straight until work measures 42 (43:44·5) cm/16½ (17:17½) in.

Shoulder shaping   Cast off 8 sts. at beg. of next 4 rows, and 5 (7:8) sts. at beg. of next 2 rows. Cast off.

Left front With 2¾ mm (No. 12) needles cast on 54 (58:62) sts. Work 10 cm (4 in) in k.1 t.b.l., p.1 rib. Change to 3¼ mm (No. 10) needles. *Next row* K. to last 12 sts., turn. Leave last 12 sts. on a safety pin. Continue in st.st. until work measures 25·5 cm (10 in), ending with a p. row.

Armhole and front shaping *Next row* Cast off 9 sts., k. to last 2 sts., k.2 tog. Dec. 1 st. at armhole edge on next 5 alternate rows, at the same time continue dec. 1 st. at front edge on every 8th row until 21 (23:24) sts. remain. Continue straight until work measures 42 (43:44·5) cm/16½ (17:17½) in, ending with a p. row.

Shoulder shaping Cast off 8 sts. at beg. of next and following alternate row. Work 1 row. Cast off.

Right front As left, reversing front border sts. and shapings.

Front borders Join shoulder seams. Sl. 12 sts. from safety pin on to 2¾ mm (No. 12) needles and continue in twisted rib as set until border fits front edge and across to centre back neck. Cast off.

Armbands Join shoulder seams. With 2¾ mm (No. 12) needles pick up and k.128 (136:144) sts. around armhole. Work 7 rows k.1 t.b.l., p.1 rib. Cast off ribwise.

Making up Press work. Sew on borders, joining ends at centre back neck. Join side seams. Sew zip fastener to centre fronts.

(7) Jacket

This is worked with double yarn throughout. It is knitted mainly in reversed stocking stitch, with huge ridged collar, patch pockets, and tie belt (see plate 3d).

Materials   43 (47:51) 25 g balls Lee Target Motoravia Double Knitting; two each 7½ mm (No. 1) and 7 mm (No. 2) knitting needles.

Measurements   To fit 86 (91:97) cm/34 (36:38) in bust; length, 71 (72: 73·5) cm/28 (28½:29) in; sleeve, 40·5 cm (16 in).

Tension   6 sts. and 8 rows to 5 cm (2 in).

Abbreviations   See page 8.

Note   Use yarn double throughout.

Back   With 7 mm (No. 2) needles cast on 62 (66:70) sts. K. 7 rows. Change to 7½ mm (No. 1) needles and continue in reverse st.st., beg. with a p. row (right side) until work measures 20 cm (8 in), ending with a k. row. Dec. 1 st. each end of next and every 10th row until 56 (60:64) sts. remain. Continue straight until work measures 51 cm (20 in), ending with a k. row.

Armhole shaping   Cast off 3 (4:4) sts. at beg. of next 2 rows. Dec. 1 st. each end of next and every alternate row until 44 (46:48) sts. remain. Continue straight until work measures 71 (72:73·5) cm/28 (28½:29) in, ending with a k. row.

Shoulder shaping   Cast off 4 (5:5) sts. at beg. of next 4 rows, 5 (4:5) sts. at beg. of following 2 rows. Cast off.

Right front   With 7 mm (No. 2) needles cast on 39 (41:43) sts. K. 7 rows. Change to 7½ mm (No. 1) needles. *1st row*   K.3, p. to end. *2nd row*   K. Keeping 3 sts. at front edge in g.st., continue in reverse st.st. until work measures 20 cm (8 in), ending with a k. row. Dec. 1 st. at end of next and every 10th row until 36 (38:40) sts. remain. Continue straight until work measures 38 cm (14¾ in), ending with a k. row.

Front shaping   Dec. 1 st. at beg. of next row and at same edge on every 3rd row until 29 (31:33) sts. remain. Work 2 rows.

Armhole shaping *Next row* Cast off 3 (4:4) sts., k. to last 2 sts., k.2 tog. Still shaping front edge as before on every 3rd row, dec. 1 st. at armhole edge on next and following 2 (2:3) alternate rows. Continue shaping front edge only until 13 (14:15) sts. remain. Work 4 (6:8) rows.

Shoulder shaping Cast off 4 (5:5) sts. at beg. of next and following alternate row. Work 1 row. Cast off.

Left front As right, reversing g.st. border and shapings.

Sleeves With 7 mm (No. 2) needles cast on 42 (46:48) sts. K. 7 rows. Change to 7½ mm (No. 1) needles and continue in reverse st.st. until work measures 40·5 cm (16 in), ending with a k. row. To shape top cast off 3 (4:4) sts. at beg. of next 2 rows. Dec. 1 st. each end of next and every alternate row until 20 sts. remain. Dec. 1 st. each end of next 4 rows. Cast off.

Collar With 7½ mm (No. 1) needles cast on 19 sts. Patt. thus: *1st row* K. *2nd row* P. *3rd and 4th rows* K. These 4 rows form patt. Continue in patt., dec. 1 st. at beg. of next and every following 4th row until 9 sts. remain. Dec. 1 st. at beg. of every alternate row until 2 sts. remain. K.2 tog. Fasten off. With right side facing pick up and k. 19 sts. along cast-on edge and work as 1st half, reversing shaping, and beg. with a 4th patt. row.

Pockets (2) With 7 mm (No. 2) needles cast on 25 sts. Change to 7½ mm (No. 1) needles. Patt. 41 rows as collar. Cast off.

Belt With 7½ mm (No. 1) needles cast on 8 sts. Work 127 cm (50 in) g.st. Cast off.

Making up Press work. Join shoulder seams. Set in sleeves. Join side and sleeve seams. Sew on collar. Sew on pockets with cast-on and cast-off edges at sides.

(8) Scoop neck sweater

This is worked throughout in a four-row lace pattern, giving it a rich textured look. It is very quick and easy to knit (see plate 3b).

Materials 17 (18:19) 25 g balls Lister Lavenda Double Knitting: two 3¾ mm (No. 9) knitting needles.

Measurements To fit 81 (86:92) cm/32 (34:36) in bust; length, 63·5 (65:66) cm/25 (25½:26) in; sleeve, 42 cm (16½ in).

Tension 10 sts. to 5 cm (2 in).

Abbreviations See page 8.

Back and front alike Cast on 84 (90:96) sts. K. 4 rows. Continue in patt. thus: *1st and 2nd rows* K.1, (k.2 tog. y.fd.) to last st., k.1. *3rd and 4th rows* K. These 4 rows form patt. Rep. patt. until work measures 46 cm (18 in).

Armhole shaping Cast off 8 (8:8) sts. at beg. of next 2 rows. Dec. 1 st. each end of next 4 rows. Continue straight until work measures 57 (58·5: 59·5) cm/22½ (23:23½) in.

Neck shaping *Next row* Patt. 23 (26:29) sts., turn. Continue on these sts. only. Dec. 1 st. at neck edge on next 8 rows. Continue straight until work measures 63·5 (65:66) cm/25 (25½:26) in, ending at armhole.

Shoulder shaping Cast off 5 (6:7) sts. at beg. of next and following 2 alternate rows. Cast off centre 14 sts. Complete other side to match.

Sleeves Cast on 36 (38:40) sts. K. 4 rows. Patt. as back, inc. 1 st. each end of 19th and every following 6th row until there are 56 (60:64) sts. Continue straight until work measures 42 cm (16½ in) approx., ending with same patt. row as main parts before armhole shaping. To shape top cast off 8 (8:8) sts. at beg. of next 2 rows. Dec. 1 st. at beg. of every row until 16 (18:20) sts. remain. Cast off 4 sts. at beg. of next 4 rows. Cast off.

Neck edging Join one shoulder. With right side facing pick up and k. 128 sts. around neck. Cast off.

Making up Press work. Join remaining shoulder. Set in sleeves. Join side and sleeve seams. Press seams.

(9) Stitch sampler jumper (plate 3c)

This is knitted in bands of ten different stitches, mainly four-row patterns, with no shaping problems. It is an easy, but interesting, practice piece.

Materials 15 (16:17:17) 25 g balls Lister/Lee Target Motoravia 4 ply; two each 3¾ mm and 3¼ mm (Nos. 9 and 10) knitting needles.

Measurements To fit 81 (86:91:97) cm/32 (34:36:38) in bust; length, 56 cm (22 in); sleeve, 15 cm (6 in).

Tension 7 sts. to 2·5 cm (1 in).

Abbreviations See plate 8.

Back With 3¼ mm (No. 10) needles cast on 122 (130:138:146) sts. Work 18 rows k.2, p.2 rib, beg. 2nd row p.2. **Scallop patt.** *1st row* K. *2nd row* P. *3rd row* P.2, (sl.1 purlwise, p.1) to end. *4th row* (P.1, k.1) to end. *5th row* K. *6th row* P. *7th row* (P.1, sl.1 purlwise) to last 2 sts., p.2. *8th row* (K.1, p.1) to end. Rep. last 8 rows twice. **Diagonal ridge patt.** *1st row* (P.1, k.3) to last 2 sts., p.1, k.1. *2nd row* P.2, (k.1, p.3) to end. *3rd row* K.2, (p.1, k.3) to end. *4th row* (K.1, p.3) to last 2 sts., k.1, p.1. Rep. last 4 rows 4 times*. **Twisted rib patt.** Change to 3¾ mm (No. 9) needles. *1st row* (K. into front of 2nd st. then into front of first st. taking both sts. off needle tog. – referred to as t.2.r., p.2) to last 2 sts., t.2.r. *2nd row* P.2, (k.2, p.2) to end. Rep. last 2 rows twice. *7th row* P.2, (t.2.r., p.2) to end. *8th row* K.2, (p.2, k.2) to end. Rep. last 2 rows twice. Rep. 1st to 6th rows once. Change to 3¼ (No. 10) needles. **Slip stitch patt.** ** *1st row* K.1, (sl.1, k.1, y.fd. and over needle to back, pass slipped st. over both the k.st. and the y.fd.) to last st., k.1. *2nd row* – P. *3rd row* K.2, rep. bracketed instructions of 1st row to last 2 sts., k.2. *4th row* P. ** Rep. last 4 rows until work measures 25·5 cm (10 in), ending with a wrong side row. **Honeycomb patt.** Change to 3¾ mm (No. 9) needles. *1st row* (T.2.r., k. into back of 2nd st. then into front of 1st st., taking both sts. off needle tog. – referred to as t.2.l.) to last 2 sts., t.2.r. *2nd row* P. *3rd row* T.2.l., (t.2.r., t.2.l.) to end. *4th row* P. Rep. last 4 rows until work measures 30·5 cm (12 in), ending with a right side

row. Change to 3¼ mm (No. 10) needles. **Wavy patt.** Rep. from ** to **
until work measures 35·5 cm (14 in), ending with a wrong side row.
Bird patt. *1st row* K. *2nd row* P. *3rd row* K.2, (p.1, p.3 tog. leaving
sts. on left-hand needle, then k. same 3 sts. tog.t.b.l., then p. same 3 sts.
tog. slipping sts. off needle, p.1, k.3) to end. *4th row* P. *5th row* K.
6th row P. *7th row* K.6, rep. bracketed instructions of 3rd row to last
4 sts., k.4. *8th row* P. Rep. last 8 rows once, then 1st to 4th rows again
***. **Arrow patt.** *1st row* K. *2nd row* K.2, (y.fd., sl.1 purlwise,
y.b.k.3) to end. *3rd row* K. *4th row* K.4, (y.fd., sl.1 purlwise, y.b.k.3) to
last 2 sts., k.2, Rep. last 4 rows 5 times, then 1st and 2nd rows again.
Ridge patt. *1st row* K. *2nd row* K.2 tog.) to end. *3rd row* K. into
front and back of each st. to end. *4th row* P. Rep. last 4 rows 5 times.
Check patt. *1st row* K.2, (p.2, k.2) to end. *2nd row* P.2, (k.2, p.2)
to end. *3rd row* As 2nd. *4th row* As 1st. Rep. last 4 rows 4 times.

Shoulder shaping *1st row* Cast off 9 (10:11:12) sts., patt. 23 (26:29:32),
k.58, patt. to end. Rep. last row once. Continue in patt., working centre
58 sts. in g.st., at the same time cast off 9 (10:11:12) sts. at beg. of next
4 rows and 10 (11:12:13) sts. at beg. of following 2 rows. Cast off remaining
48 sts.

Front As Back to ***. **Arrow patt.** *1st row* K. *2nd row* K.3, (y.fd.,
sl.1 purlwise, y.b.k.3) 8 (9:10:11) times, k.2, k.48, k.5, (y.fd., sl.1 purlwise, y.b.k.3) 8 (9:10:11) times. *3rd row* K. *4th row* K.5, (y.fd., sl.1 purlwise, y.b.k.3) 7 (8:9:10) times, k.4, k.48, k.7, (y.fd., sl.1 purlwise, y.b.k.3) 7
(8:9:10) times, k.2. Rep. last 4 rows once. *Next row* K.37 (41:45:49), cast
off 48, k. to end. Continue on last set of sts. Patt. 17 rows as set. **Ridge
patt.** *1st row* K. *2nd row* K.2 tog. to last 5 sts., k.5. *3rd row* K.5,
(k. twice into each st.) to end. *4th row* P. to last 5 sts., k.5. Rep. last 4
rows 5 times. **Check patt.** *1st row* K.5, (p.2, k.2) to end. *2nd row* (P.2,
k.2) to last 5 sts., k.5. *3rd row* K.5, (k.2, p.2) to end. *4th row* (K.2,
p.2) to last 5 sts., k.5. Rep. last 4 rows 4 times, then 1st row again.

Shoulder shaping Continue in patt. as set at the same time cast off
9 (10:11:12) sts. at beg. of next and following 2 alternate rows. Work 1
row. Cast off remaining 10 (11:12:13) sts. Rejoin yarn to inner end of
remaining sts. and complete to match first side reversing patt. rows and
shoulder shaping.

Sleeves As Back to *. Cast off.

Making up Press work. Join shoulders. Set in sleeves. Join side and
sleeve seams. Press seams.

(10) Aran bedspread and cushion covers

This bedspread is knitted in strips that are easy to carry around, and is ideal for beginners to master the art of cabling, one pattern at a time.

The stitches used are all traditional ones from the Aran islands: claw cable representing lobster claws, diamond symbolising success or wealth, honeycomb meaning hard work resulting in plenty, and cable for fisherman's ropes (see plate 4).

Materials 53 (50 g) balls Aran Knitting Wool (approximately 5 balls will knit one strip); two 5 mm (No. 6) knitting needles; cable needle.

Measurements 173 cm (68 in) wide, 218·5 cm (86 in) long, including knotted fringe.

Tension 9 sts. and 12 rows to 5 cm (2 in).

Abbreviations See page 8.

Strip A (make 6 alike) Cast on 24 sts. *1st row* Place right-hand needle under then over yarn (to make a loop st. over needle – referred to as 'm.1'), k.2 tog., k.2, p.2, k.12, p.2, k.4. *2nd row* M.1, k.2 tog., k.4, p.12, k.6. *3rd row* M.1, k.2 tog., k.2, p.2, sl. next 3 sts. onto cable needle and leave at back of work, k.3 then k. 3 sts. from cable needle – referred to as 'cable 6 right' (c.6.r.), sl. 3 sts. onto cable needle and leave at front of work, k.3, then k. sts. from cable needle – referred to as 'cable 6 left' (c.6.l.), p.2, k.4. Rep. 2nd row, then rep. 1st and 2nd rows 4 times. These 12 rows form patt. Continue in patt. until strip measures 218·5 cm (86 in), ending with a 5th patt. row. Cast off.

Strip B (make 2 alike) Cast on 28 sts. *1st row* M.1, k.2 tog., k.2, p.2, *k. into front of 2nd st. on left-hand needle, then k. into 1st st. and drop both sts. off left-hand needle – referred to as 'twist 2 right' (t.2.r.); k. into back of 2nd st. on left-hand needle, then k. into 1st st. and drop both sts. off left-hand needle – referred to as 'twist 2 left' (t.2.l.); rep. from * 3 times, p.2, k.4. *2nd row* M.1, k.2 tog., k.4, p.16, k.6. *3rd row* M.1, k.2 tog., k.2, p.2, (t.2.l., t.2.r.) 4 times, p.2, k.4. *4th row* As 2nd. These 4 rows form patt. Continue in patt. until strip measures 218·5 cm (86 in), ending with a 3rd patt. row. Cast off.

Strip C (make 2 alike)   Cast on 25 sts. *1st row*   M.1, k.2 tog., k.2, p.8, into next st. work k.1 (y.r.n., k.1) twice into next st. – referred to as 'work 5 in 1', p.8, k.4. *2nd and every alternate row*   M.1, k.2 tog., k. to end. *3rd row*   M.1, k.2 tog., k.2, p.8, p.2 tog., p.3 tog., pass 2nd st. over first on right-hand needle – referred to as 'work 5 tog.', p.8, k.4.

Note   one cluster pattern completed in centre over the 4 rows. *5th row*   M.1, k.2 tog., k.2, p.7, work 5 in 1, k.1, 5 in 1, p.7, k.4. *7th row* M.1, k.2 tog., k.2, p.7, work 5 tog., k.1, work 5 tog., p.7, k.4. *9th row*   M.1, k.2 tog., k.2, p.6, work 5 in 1, (k.1 work 5 in 1) twice, p.6, k.4. *11th row*   M.1, k.2 tog., k.2, p.6, work 5 tog., (k.1, work 5 tog.) twice, p.6, k.4. Continue in this way, working one more cluster over every 4 rows until there are 7 clusters. *29th row*   M.1, k.2 tog., k.2, p.3, work 5 in 1, (k.1, 5 in 1) 5 times, p.3, k.4. Continue in patt. dec. 1 cluster every 4 rows until 1 cluster remains. These 52 rows complete diamond patt. Rep. patt. until strip measures 218·5 cm (86 in) ending with a 3rd patt. row. Cast off.

Strip D   Cast on 28 sts. *1st row* (wrong side)   M.1, k.2 tog., k.6, (p.4, k.4) twice, k.4. *2nd row*   M.1, k.2 tog., k.2, p.4, sl. next 2 sts. onto cable needle and leave at back of work, k.2, then k.2 from cable needle – referred to as 'cable 4 right' (c.4.r.), p.4, sl. next 2 sts. onto cable needle and leave at front of work, k.2, then k.2 from cable needle – referred to as 'cable 4 left' (c.4.l.), p.4, k.4. *3rd row*   As 1st row. *4th row*   M.1, k.2 tog., k.2, p.3, sl. next st. onto cable needle and leave at back of work, k.2, then p. st. from cable needle – referred to as 'twist 3 right' (t.3.r.), sl. next 2 sts. onto cable needle and leave at front of work, p.1, then k.2 from cable needle – referred to as 'twist 3 left' (t.3.l.), p.2, t.3.r., t.3.l., p.3, k.4. *5th row*   M.1, k.2 tog. k.5, (p.2, k.2) 4 times, k.5. *6th row*   M.1, k.2 tog., k.2, p.2 (t.3.r., p.2, t.3.l.) twice, p.2, k.4. *7th row*   M.1, k.2 tog., k.4 (p.2, k.4, p.2) twice, k.6. *8th row*   M.1, k.2 tog., k.2, p.2, k.2, p.4, c.4.r., p.4, k.2, p.2, k.4. *9th row*   As 7th row. *10th row*   M.1, k.2 tog., k.2, p.2, k.2, p.4, k.4, p.4, k.2, p.2, k.4. Rep. 7th and 8th rows then 7th row again. *14th row*   M.1, k.2 tog., k.2, p.2 (t.3.l., p.2, t.3.r.) twice, p.2, k.4. *15th row*   As 5th row. *16th row*   M.1, k.2 tog., k.2, p.3, t.3.l., t.3.r., p.2, t.3.l., t.3.r., p.3, k.4. *17th row*   M.1, k.2 tog., k.6, (p.4, k.4) twice, k.4. *18th row*   As 2nd row. *19th row*   As 17th row. *20th row*   As 4th row. *21st row*   M.1, k.2 tog., k.5, (p.2, k.2) 4 times, k.5. *22nd row*   M.1, k.2 tog., k.2, p.3, (k.2, p.2) twice, k.2, sl. last 6 sts. of the 15 sts. just worked onto cable needle and wind yarn anti-clockwise 4 times around these 6 sts., sl. the 6 sts. back onto right-hand needle, p.2, k.2, p.3, k.4. *23rd row*   M.1, k.2 tog., k.5, (p.2, k.2) 4 times, k.5. *24th row* M.1, k.2 tog., k.2, p.3, t.3.l., t.3.r., p.2, t.3.l., t.3.r., p.3, k.4. These 24 rows form patt. Continue in patt. until strip measures 218·5 cm (86 in) ending with a 24th patt. row. Cast off.

Making up Press strips on wrong side with a warm iron over a damp cloth. Join strips together as shown in plan (Figure 98).

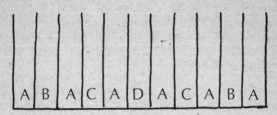

Figure 98

Using yarn double throughout k. and cast off seams thus: * insert needle through parallel loops on strips and draw st. through; rep. from * then sl. 2nd st. over first (as for cast-off); rep. from * to end. Draw yarn through final st. to fasten off.

Fringe Cut yarn into 37 cm (14½ in) lengths, winding around card or book with this measurement. Using a crochet hook knot 4 strands through every alternate loop st. at sides and 1·5 cm (½ in) apart along lower edge.

*Knot 2 strands from each group together 2·5 cm (1 in) apart; rep. from * then trim ends to neaten fringe.

Square cushion cover in Trinity stitch

Materials 5 balls (50 g) Lister/Lee Target Aran; two 5½ mm (No. 5) knitting needles.

Measurement 41 cm (16 in) square.

Tension 5 sts. to 2·5 cm (1 in).

Abbreviations See page 8.

The square (make 2 alike). Cast on 80 sts. *1st row* (right side) P. *2nd row* *P.3 tog., (k.1, p.1, k.1) in next st.; rep. from * to end. *3rd row* P. *4th row* * (K.1, p.1, k.1) in next st., p.3 tog.; rep. from * to end. These 4 rows form patt. Continue in patt. until work measures 41 cm (16 in). Cast off.

Making up Press work. Join 3 sides, insert pad then join remaining side, or insert zip fastener.

Rectangular cushion cover   (can be used to cover a pillow.)

Materials   7 balls (50 g) Lister/Lee Target Aran; two 5½ mm (No. 5) knitting needles.

Measurements   41 cm (16 in) by 61 cm (24 in).

Tension   5 sts. to 2·5 cm (1 in).

Abbreviations   See page 8.

The rectangle (make 2 alike)   Cast on 80 sts. *1st and 2nd rows*   (K.1, p.1) to end. *3rd and 4th rows*   (P.1, k.1) to end. These 4 rows form patt. Continue in patt. until work measures 61 cm (24 in). Cast off.

Making up   As square cover.

7 Renovations and after care

The cost of materials, and the time spent in the knitting, makes every garment too precious to discard. Good quality yarns can always be unravelled and re-used when garments have to be brought up to date, or remade for growing children.

Knowing how to pull a thread, and how to graft, makes every kind of alteration possible, and besides the brand new lease of life for a favourite old knitted garment, there's the satisfaction of saving money.

Endless renovations are possible for too-good-to-throw-away knitteds and a few of these are illustrated, with ideas for using up oddments too.

Basic repairs

Keep scraps of every yarn you use for darning holes, sewing on buttons, or renovations.

Oddments
Left-over yarn can be put to good use for scarves and other accessories – and also for knitting toys. Very fine yarns can be used two or three-fold to make up the thickness required, and textured yarns enhance the overall effect, especially for cushions and bedspreads.

Worn welts
Re-knit worn welts and cuffs by pulling a thread above these and re-knitting them downwards.

Worn edges re-inforced
To conceal edges that have worn or pulled out of shape, bind them and add a patch pocket of the same fabric.

Stretched ribbing
Revive stretched ribbing by threading shirring elastic through alternate ridges on the wrong side.

Holes

Mend holes before they get beyond repair – as soon as there is a broken thread. Darn over the break with matching yarn, working chain stitch to the same tension as the knitted fabric.

Unravelling

Unpick all seams, being careful not to snip the knitting. Unravel from the cast-off edge (it cannot be done in the opposite direction) pulling gently to disengage the loops. Discard sections that have worn thin – check this by holding the knitting against the light. As the yarn is released wind it to form a skein around a tray or straight furniture. Tie each end of the skein. Wet the skein thoroughly and hang it up to dry, weighting it to remove crinkles. Rewind into a loose ball for re-knitting.

Re-knitting

Use unravelled yarn differently – for instance, use yarn from the back for the sleeves to re-distribute the wear. Allowing for discarded yarn, make a smaller size garment, or add contrast to make up the amount.

Alternatively, make accessories or amalgamate yarns for an oddments garment – all textures can be used as long as they knit to the right tension.

Square from scraps

This is knitted diagonally to keep it in good shape when sewn into a blanket – the weight pulls evenly in all directions and the garter stitch will not distort readily. Also, it forms attractive chevron (v-shaped) patterns if worked in stripes.

Use double knitting yarn and two $3\frac{3}{4}$ mm (No. 9) knitting needles and a 25 g ball will knit four 8 cm ($3\frac{1}{4}$ in) squares. (For abbreviations see page 8.)

Cast on 1 st. *1st row*   Inc. *2nd row*   K.1, inc. in next st. *3rd row*   K.1, inc. in next st., k. to end. Rep. last row until there are 25 sts. *Next row*   K.1, k.2 tog., k. to end. Rep. last row until 2 sts. remain. K.2 tog. Fasten off. Sew squares together edge to edge.

Improving a jumper or cardigan

Basic jumper or cardigan (indicated by dotted line) to be renovated because of tired looks or worn out areas (Figure 99).

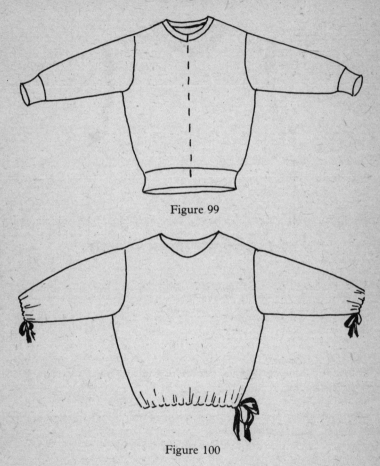

Figure 99

Figure 100

Drawstring top   Remove welts and cuffs by pulling a thread above these (see Figure 105). Turn in narrow hems, or use bought hem facing if maximum lengths are needed, at sleeve and lower edges. Thread drawstrings through hems and bring these out through small openings in the seams to tie.

Figure 101 – Slipover

Slipover   Remove welts and sleeves (or armbands) and neckband. Bind edges as shown in Figures 102 a and b.

Fabric binding   Use bias fabric in a contrasting colour or left over from a dress, so that the slipover will co-ordinate.

(a) Sew binding to right side of knitted fabric (Figure 102a).

(b) Turn binding to wrong side and slip-stitch over seam (Figure 102b).

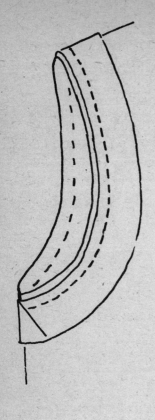

Figure 102a

Figure 102b

Figure 103 – Short-sleeved jumper

Short-sleeved jumper Open sleeve seam and pull a thread at length required, allowing 2·5 cm (1 in) for ribbing (see Figure 105). Pick up stitches and knit matching rib. Cast off ribwise. Join sleeve seam.

Alternatively, unravel and re-knit the jumper in the lacy pattern shown in diagram to give it a very new look.

Bell lace pattern
Stitches must be divisible by 6, minus 1. For abbreviations see page 8.
1st row (P.2, k.1, p.2, y.r.n., k.1, y.r.n.) to last 5 sts., p.2, k.1, p.2.
2nd row (K.2, p.1, k.2, p.3) to last 5 sts., k.2, p.1, k.2. *3rd row* (P.2, k.1, p.2, k.3) to last 5 sts., p.2, k.1, p.2. Rep. 2nd and 3rd rows. *6th row* (K.2, p.1, k.2, p.3 tog.) to last 5 sts., k.2, p.1, k.2. *7th row* (P.2, y.r.n., k.1, y.r.n., p.2, k.1) to end, omitting k.1 at end. *8th row* (K.2, p.3, k.2, p.1) to end, omitting p.1 at end. *9th row* (P.2, k.3, p.2, k.1) to end, omitting k.1 at end. Rep. 8th and 9th rows. *12th row* (K.2, p.3 tog., k.2, p.1) to end, omitting p.1 at end. These 12 rows form pattern.

Figure 104 – Quilted yoke

Quilted yoke   Replace worn sections. Pull a thread below the armholes and straight across the sleeves. Cast off stitches. Use the yoke sections that were removed to cut out the quilted fabric, disregarding the armhole shaping. Sew yoke to jumper and sew sleeves to the straight edges.

This renovation could also be done in leather, or the worn sections re-knitted in contrast yarn.

Pulling a thread

Cut yarn at the end of the row and draw the cut thread until the knitted fabric puckers. Keep cutting the thread so that the knitted stitches are released on either side, a few at a time, as shown in diagram. Finally cut the same thread at the end of the row. Use a smaller size needle to pick up the released stitches purlwise.

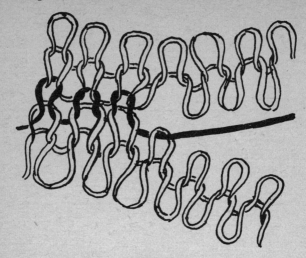

Figure 105

Lengthening, shortening and widening

To lengthen garment
Pull a thread immediately above the welt. Knit the extra rows required on to the lower released stitches. Finally graft the stitches together (see Figure 106).

To widen garment
To widen a garment inset side panels of contrast. Extend these insets up to shoulder level when no armhole shaping is involved, then sew sleeve top underneath the extension.

   Inset panels of knitted lace to enlarge garments. Machine stitch knitted fabric either side of the line to be cut for insertion.

To shorten garment
Pull a thread immediately above the number of rows to be unravelled. This can only be done downwards from the direction of knitting (from cast off edge). Unravel the rows, then graft welt back into position (see Figure 105).

Grafting
It is most useful to know how to graft stitches as this makes all kinds of alterations possible. Pieces of knitting can be joined so that no seam

is visible – the grafting forms a row of stitches indistinguishable from the fabric created on the knitting needles. Grafting needs to be done to the same tension as the knitted stitches – the sewn-in loops must not be drawn up too tightly, and the loops should be even throughout (Figure 106).

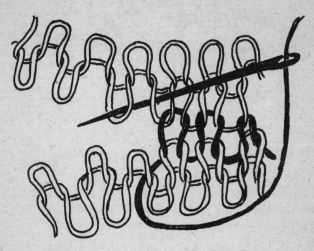

Figure 106

Flat grafting

It is easier to do this with the knitted sections placed together horizontally on a flat surface, with the knit side uppermost. Use a wool needle and a long strand of the yarn. Weave the needle in and out twice through each loop as shown, connecting the stitches as though the knitting was continuous.

Alternatively, stitches can be grafted directly off the knitting needles, placed side by side with the wrong side of the work inside (Figure 107).

Take the threaded wool needle through the stitch on the front needle purlwise, but do not drop this off the knitting needle. Take wool needle through the back stitch knitwise, but do not drop this off the knitting needle. *Take the wool needle through the front needle stitch knitwise and drop this stitch off the knitting needle, then take the wool needle through the next stitch on the front needle purlwise, but do not drop this stitch off the knitting needle; take the wool needle through the back needle stitch purlwise and drop this stitch off the knitting needle, then take the wool

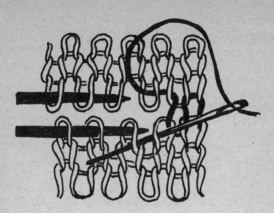

Figure 107

needle through the next stitch on the back needle knitwise but do not drop
this stitch off the needle; repeat this double weaving from * until all the
knitted stitches have been grafted together, working the final knit and purl
stitches off singly.

Lengthening stripes
Insert contrast stripes to make up the required length by pulling threads
(Figure 105) and grafting (Figure 106).

Lengthening Fair Isle
If insufficient matching yarn is available for the length required, use a
contrasting colour and work a Fair Isle pattern – this method also disguises
differing dye lots too. See Figures 105 and 106 for pulling a thread and
grafting.

Button-up cardigan into bolero
Remove welts, sleeves, front and neckband. Bind edges with fabric, using
bias fabric and mitreing corners (see Figure 102).
   An alternative to fabric binding is blanket stitching. Work this evenly
around all the edges.

Blanket stitch
Use a wool needle and yarn of the same thickness as the knitted fabric.
Keep the embroidery even by working through the same row of knitting
and an equal number of stitches apart (Figure 108).

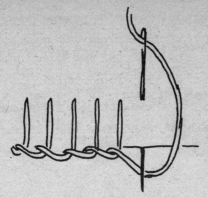

Figure 108

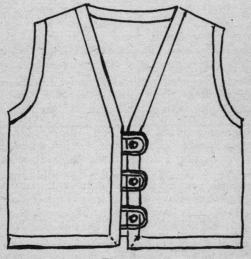

Figure 109

Button-low cardigan into waistcoat

Remove welts, sleeves and front bands. Bind edges and add rouleau (round) loops for button fastening (Figure 109).

Jumpers can also be converted into cardigans. Machine stitch two or three times each side of centre front, leaving a 1 cm ($\frac{1}{2}$ in) channel between the rows of stitching. Cut through the channel and bind the cut edges.

Washing and storing

It is a good idea to keep one ball-band of the yarn to refer to for care instructions and to tie this with a length of the relevant yarn for easy identification.

do not iron   do not bleach   do not dry-clean

Figure 110

Figure 110 shows the principal symbols and their meanings.

Washing
It is always safest to hand wash if this is possible. Turn the garment inside out to minimise surface disturbance. Dissolve the washing solution in lukewarm water before immersing the garment. Do not rub knitted fabric – squeeze it gently without lifting it out of the water. Rinse in the same temperature water until water is quite clear.

Machine washing
Follow the care symbols on the yarn band and match the machine programme to the symbols. Use the machine on a gentle cycle and watch the temperature of the water. Do not tumble dry but place in a pillow case and spin dry to remove any moisture.

Drying
Roll the garment in a towel to remove excess moisture. Place it on a flat surface and pat it into shape, especially ribbing, then leave it to dry thoroughly. Never hang a knitted garment up to dry and do not leave it in a strong sun – this affects the colour (white is particularly vulnerable to discolouration). Do not dry near heat – this causes matting and shrinkage.

Storing
Knitted garments should be folded and stored flat. Never hang them.

Fluffy yarns (such as mohair and Angora)
After washing these shake the garment from time to time during the drying process to restore the fluffiness of the yarn.

8 Comparison tables

Comparative sizes of knitting needles

American	English		Continental
	Metric	Imperial	(millimetres)
00	2	14	2
0	$2\frac{1}{4}$	13	
1	$2\frac{3}{4}$	12	$2\frac{1}{2}$
2	3	11	3
3	$3\frac{1}{4}$	10	
4	$3\frac{3}{4}$	9	$3\frac{1}{2}$
5	4	8	4
6	$4\frac{1}{2}$	7	$4\frac{1}{2}$
7	5	6	5
8	$5\frac{1}{2}$	5	$5\frac{1}{2}$
9	6	4	6
10	$6\frac{1}{2}$	3	$6\frac{1}{2}$
$10\frac{1}{2}$	7	2	7
11	$7\frac{1}{2}$	1	$7\frac{1}{2}$
12	8	0	8
13	9	00	9
15	10	000	10

Yarn Equivalents

	America	Australia	South Africa
3 ply	*Lister/Lee Target*	*Patons*	*Patons*
	Nursery Time 3 ply	Azalea	Silversheen 3 ply
	EasyWash Baby 3 ply	Feather Soft 3 ply	Fairytale 3 ply
		Sirdar	*Sirdar*
		Wonderland 3 ply	Snuggly 3 ply
		Baby Speckle	Wonderland Twinkle 3 ply
		Spun 3 ply	*Lister/Lee Target*
			EasyWash Baby 3 ply
4 ply	*Lister/Lee Target*	*Sirdar*	*Patons*
	EasyWash 4 ply	Fontein Crepe 4 ply	Bluebell Cameo Crepe
		Wonderland 4 ply	Go-Go Baby 4 ply
			Gala 4 ply
		Lister/Lee Target	*Sirdar*
		Tricel/Nylon 4 ply	Superwash 4 ply Crepe
			Snuggly
			Courtelle 4 ply Crepe
			Lister/Lee Target
			Lavenda Crepe 4 ply
			EasyWash 4 ply Crepe
Double Knitting	*Lister/Lee Target*	*Sirdar*	*Patons*
	Fashion Tweed D.K.	Cottage Craft	Gala Double Knitting
	EasyWash Tweed D.K.	Double Crepe	Gem Stone Double Knitting
	Superwash Wool D.K.	*Lister/Lee Target*	Fairytale D.K.
		Fashion Tweed D.K.	*Sirdar*
		Superwash Wool D.K.	Superwash Double Crepe
			Snuggly
			Courtelle Double Crepe
			Lister/Lee Target
			Fashion Tweed D.K.
			EasyWash D.K.
Aran	*Lister/Lee Target*	*Sirdar*	*Patons*
	Spec. Qual. for Aran	Sports Wool	Capstan
	Bernat	*Lister/Lee Target*	*Sirdar*
	Blarney Spun	Irish Spun for Aran	Sherpa
		Spec. Qual. for Aran	
Mohair	*Lister/Lee Target*	*Sirdar*	*Patons*
	Tahiti	Moonmist	Mohair Spun
	Bernat		
	Mohair Plus		

Note: Always check tension of interchanged qualites.

Tension guide

This is only a guide (stitches and rows to 2·5 cm (1 in)), as measurements vary according to the stitch used. The correct tension is given in every pattern.

Needle size		3 ply thickness		4 ply thickness		double knitting thickness	
mm	No.	stitches	rows	stitches	rows	stitches	rows
5	6	$5\frac{1}{2}$	$7\frac{1}{2}$	5	7	$4\frac{1}{2}$	$6\frac{1}{2}$
$4\frac{1}{2}$	7	6	8	$5\frac{1}{2}$	$7\frac{1}{2}$	5	7
4	8	$6\frac{1}{2}$	$8\frac{1}{2}$	6	8	$5\frac{1}{2}$	$7\frac{1}{2}$
$3\frac{3}{4}$	9	7	9	$6\frac{1}{2}$	$8\frac{1}{2}$	6	8
$3\frac{1}{4}$	10	$7\frac{1}{2}$	$9\frac{1}{2}$	7	9	$6\frac{1}{2}$	$8\frac{1}{2}$
3	11	8	10	$7\frac{1}{2}$	$9\frac{1}{2}$	7	9
$2\frac{1}{2}$	12	$8\frac{1}{2}$	$10\frac{1}{2}$	8	10	$7\frac{1}{2}$	$9\frac{1}{2}$

Weight comparison chart

A useful guide of approximate conversions if old patterns or yarns are being used.

Grammes	Ounces
20	·7
25	·9
30	1·05
40	1·4
50	1·75
100	3·50

Strictly accurate: 28·347 grammes equals 1 ounce.

Equivalent measurements

centimetres	51	56	61	66	71	76	81	86	91
inches	20	22	24	26	28	30	32	34	36

centimetres	97	102	107	112	117
inches	38	40	42	44	46

Index

CROCHET

JEAN KINMOND

With this well-illustrated guide to Crochet you will quickly master this versatile and attractive craft—ideal for fashion garments and home decorations.

Basic stitches are shown in easy to follow instructions to make up the wide range of attractive patterns. Different uses to which crochet can be put include making shawls, blouses and table cloths, and will provide stimulating ideas for the expert and beginner alike.

Jean Kinmond was Needlecraft and Fashion adviser to Coats, the internationally known threadmakers, for many years.

TEACH YOURSELF BOOKS

DRESSMAKING

ISABEL HORNER

Dressmaking can be a very enjoyable way of keeping yourself in fashionable but inexpensive clothes. It can also be a way of appearing in a dress that only too obviously has been 'run up in a few hours'.

With this book even the beginner can avoid the usual pitfalls of home dressmaking and will be able to make very attractive, yet economical clothes.

Initial chapters on equipment, patterns and materials are followed by step-by-step instructions on each stage of dressmaking: cutting out, tacking up, fitting, fastenings, trimmings etc. The author also includes advice on renovation and remodelling and the care and repair of clothes.

Although intended primarily for the beginner, this book will be useful as a source of reference and ideas to the more experienced dressmaker.

TEACH YOURSELF BOOKS

CREATIVE CRAFTS

FREDERICK OUGHTON

This book has been designed as a bank of ideas about craft methods and materials, to start the reader thinking, looking, perceiving and *doing* using only cheap or free materials.

The contents cover a wide field of craft materials and techniques, including paper, plaster, wood and clay, modelling, moulding, carving and design. The emphasis throughout is on explaining the basics of each craft, on starting points for the beginner and on finding fun and self-expression in craft work.

Packed with ideas, advice and information, this book will provide just the stimulus needed by anyone who wants to get started in creative crafts but doesn't quite know where to begin.

TEACH YOURSELF BOOKS

EMBROIDERY

LYNETTE DE DENNE

Embroidery is a very ancient and beautiful art using many different techniques which reflect the life of the periods in which they were developed. Today, the embroiderer can make use of all these different styles and produce work of great variety and originality, often by mixing techniques: patchwork can appear as part of a wall hanging, canvas work be applied to another background with other stitchery.

This book gives clear step-by-step instructions on the different techniques and how they can be used and is fully illustrated throughout. Lynette de Denne has also included useful advice on buying material and threads and ideas for making your own embroidery designs.

This is the basis the beginner needs when starting to embroider and with it you will be able to find out what you enjoy most and to start adapting or combining the different techniques to your individual designs. A well-planned, simple embroidery can often be as effective as intricate and sophisticated work.

Lynette de Denne is an Embroidery Consultant and an editor of *Embroidery*.

TEACH YOURSELF BOOKS